Teaching History Today

A Selection of Articles
from the Column "Teaching History Today"
Published in the Newsletter of
the American Historical Association
1974–1984

Editor: Henry S. Bausum
Virginia Military Institute

American Historical Association
institutional services program

© American Historical Association, 1985
ISBN: 0–87229–034–4
Library of Congress catalog card number: 85–73224

PREFACE

The teaching of history was rarely a subject of discussion at annual meetings of the American Historical Association before 1970. One of the first sessions, a program on introductory history, attracted a standing-room-only audience in 1971, and programs on teaching have since been regular and increasingly important features of AHA annual meetings. Coinciding with this has been a growing awareness by AHA leaders of the importance of classroom teaching. "Teaching History Today," a column appearing regularly for more than a decade in AHA Perspectives, or its predecessor AHA Newsletter, has been influential in extending that awareness and in keeping the interest in teaching alive.

Since this book is a selection from columns written between 1974 and 1984, and since those columns include some of the most perceptive comments made on history teaching in recent decades, I am indebted foremost--as a former editor of the column and as editor of this book--to the hundreds of historians who submitted columns during those years. All of us who have read and appreciated the column over the years are indebted to William H. McNeill who arranged for the column's publication. I am personally appreciative of the willingness and competence with which the present editors of "Teaching History Today," Mildred Alpern and Jeanette Lauer, and a former editor, Myron Marty, assisted in selecting columns for this collection. I am also grateful for the prompt and useful responses by contributors to the book.

I undertook the project primarily because of encouragement by Myron Marty and the support of Jamil Zainaldin, Deputy Executive Director of the American Historical Association. I was fortunate in having the competent help at VMI of Anita Fuller and Janet Aldridge and the valuable editorial support at the AHA of Maureen Vincent-Morgan and Simon Cordery. The patient assistance of my wife has also been invaluable in seeking to turn out an accurate camera-ready copy of the manuscript. Finally, I am indebted to the Virginia Military Institute for its support and to the Teaching Division of the American Historical Association for its sponsorship of the project.

CONTENTS

INTRODUCTION

In the spring of 1974, fifteen historians met for two conferences in Lexington, Virginia to discuss the prospects in American colleges and universities for introductory history. They came from major universities-- Chicago, Princeton, MIT, Michigan, UNC, and Duke--as well as from institutions of lesser renown. Although Western Civilization courses at the time were declining, the persons who met in Lexington saw little or no likelihood that historians could reach a consensus on an alternative course. In a pluralistic society, so the argument went, we must contend with multiple approaches to history.

One thing on which all of us could agree, however, was the need for discussion of all aspects of history teaching. William H. McNeill, who directed the transition in 1974 from the old AHA Committee on Teaching to the new Teaching Division, attended the conferences in Lexington, and arranged after them to have space set aside in the AHA_Newsletter for a column on teaching. Subsequently, he asked Myron Marty and me to edit the series beginning with the September issue in 1974. The series began under the title, "Innovation in History," and first appeared under its present title, "Teaching History Today," in September 1975.

The column appeared regularly in each issue of the AHA Newsletter until 1981 when demands on space prevented its publication. Since 1981, it has continued to appear in most issues of the Newsletter or its successor, AHA_Perspectives. During the period 1974-1984 more than a hundred persons contributed individually or jointly to the column, and although the influence of the column cannot be easily assessed, its very presence has had the effect of lending dignity to the teaching role of historians.

The column began as a collection of short statements which reflected activity already astir in many colleges and universities and awareness that we could not as a profession proceed as though nothing had changed. One of the early statements which helped set the tone of the columns described the decision by Gordon Craig, Lewis Spitz, and Gordon Wright to contribute their prestige and expertise to the teaching of Western Civilization at Stanford University. Their involvement led ultimately to the reinstatement of a history requirement at Stanford and served as a much needed model for young professors at numerous small colleges and universities who had previously felt themselves trapped in the introductory Western Civilization program.

When Marty and I first began editing the column, we agreed that in selecting manuscripts for publication, we would seek statements giving positive and constructive direction to the profession. We felt it important that historians gain confidence from their teaching as well as their research activity, and we felt it important to emphasize the possibilities before the profession rather than lament the supposed crisis which some were describing as the demise of history.

During the course of the first decade of the column, topics were rarely repeated. Of the 74 full-length columns appearing between September 1975 and May/June 1984, about 30 dealt with pedagogical approaches, 10 with curriculum, another 10 with the status of the profession, and the remainder with such diverse topics as evaluation, textbooks, social studies, and the techniques of presenting history to an audience. The diversity of pedagogical approaches is particularly interesting and the reader might profitably spend a few brief moments reviewing the entire list of columns in the appendix to this volume.

I have organized the present group of columns under six topics, a structure which emerged only after all selections had been made. I aim to focus on the fact that the subject matter of teaching history has more than one dimension, a fact demonstrated not only in the columns selected for this publication, but also by the wide variety of emphases in the total collection of columns.

The first topic, "Teaching History," is best represented by a column written by Norman A. Graebner. Good teaching, contends Graebner, is not an accident; the challenge is to bring a class alive in a "rising spiral of intellectual and emotional interaction," a totally satisfying student-professor relationship.

The second topic, "Introducing History to College Students," sets forth four possible approaches for introductory history. E. Bradford Burns discusses in "Teaching History: A Changing Clientele and an Affirmation of Goals" a number of trends in academe and in the history profession, and suggests how we need to recognize and reject certain myths which prevent us from correcting or coping with entrenched trends in the way we do things. Professor McNeill argues persuasively that what is needed in an introductory history course "is clear thinking about what is really important in defining public identities and behavior in the world today." From this imperative emerges his emphasis on World History. Evelyn Edson, who entered the ranks of Western Civilization at Chicago in the 1960's, makes a plea for an introductory history based on the Western experience, an experience, she says, with which most students have little historical consciousness, "an intellectual world that has formerly been closed" to them. Finally, I argue in "The Social Function of History" for the need to take a fresh look at introductory history, a need justified by the enormous changes which have taken place in contemporary society as well as by the expansion in recent decades of the subject matter of history.

Our third topic is "History and the Public Schools." A column by Lester D. Stephens, "From History to Social Studies," represents this emphasis. Stephens reviews the AHA efforts early in this century to upgrade history in the public schools and the emergence of the social studies, and argues that excellent history teachers are still needed in our secondary schools--teachers who have acquired a historian's sense of the past.

Intermixed with columns on curriculum and faculty competence have been a large number on the techniques of teaching history. We reprint under our fourth topic, "Techniques in Teaching History," columns dealing with five of these approaches--film, methodology, the use of accessible primary sources, oral history, and use of the library. John E. O'Connor, in "Film Study and the History Classroom," illustrates how films can help "train students to comprehend more fully the popular media of the present." Julie Thompson Klein explains in "To Begin With . . . Excercises in Historiography," how students can gain "intellectual sensitivities which serve them beyond their ...school days." In "Using Primary Sources in Teaching Social History," Patricia Ebrey sets forth precise examples of ways in which teachers can make use of readily available sources--deeds, contracts, ordinances, agreements--to help students experience the excitement of discovery and interpretation. Jacqueline B. Barnhart, in "Doing Oral History: the Yountville Project," describes how an application of oral history helped students in a course grasp the fact that "not only is history interpretive, but historical memory also varies according to one's perspective." Finally, E.A. Reitan discusses in his essay, "New Perspectives on Using the Library in History Teaching," some results of a workshop involving history faculty and library staff. Students, he says, are often intimidated by the library and do not know how to use it. Teachers, therefore, need to spell out precise steps which students should follow in carrying out their library research.

The fourth topic, "The New History," focuses on two areas of history which have gained wide expression in the past couple of decades. Few historians today would question the statement made by Gerda Lerner in "Teaching Women's History" that "the long neglect of women in history reflects cultural neglect;" a reversal of this pattern--because of its serious long-range effect on women and indeed on society at large--is unquestionably long overdue. Thad W. Tate's column, "Problems of Definition in Environmental History," is written in the hope that environmental history--a theme which may sometimes seem today to contribute to a fragmentation of history--will "eventuate in a new and richer synthesis of historical understanding." He argues that advocacy and present-mindedness, so characteristic of many environmental studies, place on the environmental historian "an unusually strong demand for reasonable detachment and objectivity and for a sense of historical perspective."

The final section, "The Condition of History in the

Classroom," is an approppriate concluding statement by Myron Marty entitled "Illusions." With his characteristic forthrightness he brings us face to face with the mental blocks standing between us, as teaching members of the history profession, and reality--"Illusions," as he puts it, preventing us from necessary self-assessment and action. We have a responsibility, he says, to see to it that some part of the experience of those caught up in the scramble to acquire "entry-level skills" be devoted to history, a task demanding of the history teacher "that every muscle be stretched to make the experience beneficial to students."

Selecting the columns for publication in this collection was not an easy task. It was undertaken by a committee of the past and present editors of the column. Together we sought to select columns both representative and meaningful, columns accurately reflecting the best of "Teaching History Today." We found agreement on some of the columns at first reading. Other choices surfaced more slowly as we became aware that most of the articles were, in fact, well done and that many of them had a timeless quality.

I would be remiss if I did not admit to a measure of subjectivity in making the selections for this volume. As I look over the list of omissions, I have regrets--as those of you who have followed the column over the years may have when you find your favorite column missing from this collection--that we could not be more inclusive. The editor asks for the forbearance of readers and hopes that whatever disappointment is felt by the omission of favorite columns may be tempered by tolerance. The reader may discover by reading or rereading these selections--as the editor has in working with them--reason to renew yet once again a resolve to pursue excellence in the teaching of history.

July 1985   HSB

I. TEACHING HISTORY

OBSERVATIONS ON UNIVERSITY TEACHING AND RESEARCH

Norman A. Graebner

December 1975

Good teaching does not happen accidentally. Making it happen is the responsibility of the university faculty--but it is not the responsibility of the faculty alone. I know that although every university worthy of the name holds teaching in high regard and is willing to reward it when it becomes measurable, university officials generally have not advertised this fact and rather have, by their policies and their acclaim, suggested strongly and often that those who conduct successful research and publish their findings shall be the special inheritors of the earth. Only rarely is the national and international reputation of a university determined by the level of teaching performance in its classrooms. Were teaching held in higher regard in the words and actions of university leaders, so that the rewards for it in both acclaim and monetary compensation were clearly demonstrated, there would be a higher level of teaching endeavor.

At the conclusion of an honors convocation at one of the New York universities a disillusioned student asked me what that university might do to secure better teaching. In my response I suggested that a half dozen $25,000 teaching professorships might help immeasurably. Members of university faculties are quite conscious of their interests, and when those interests become attached to some marked improvement in classroom performance, at least some will respond. It is for this reason that I am pleased to see any institution's efforts to improve its teaching function. Alliances between professors and administrators need to be cultivated.

Throughout my years of college and university education, the teaching I experienced at every level and in every discipline was often not what it should have been--although I have had my share of excellent instruction, especially at the graduate level. It was not strange that the student rebellion of the sixties fo-

cused in part on what it regarded as the over-emphasis
of at least the major universities on research and writing. If it is true that the faculties of the noted universities are the most talented and have the lightest
teaching loads, they should have had both the time and
the capabilities to teach superbly.

In part the challenge to good teaching rests with
departments which can insist on good classroom performance in their decision for promotion and tenure. During
a quarter century of teaching in a number of major universities I have never attended a meeting in which
teaching was the primary subject of conversation. University departments, like university administrations,
take at least adequate teaching for granted, and certainly many of them, through no special effort, achieve
and maintain an acceptable level of instruction. What
matters in departmental decisions is publication or the
promise of publication. Frankly, I favor such publication. Without some consistent program of research and
writing, a non-administrative member of a university
department can quickly turn an appointment into a sine-
cure. Inasmuch as a department, except for rare occa-
sions, never purposely promotes a colleague to tenure
who is not a good teacher, every member of every university faculty is a good teacher at least on one day of
his or her life, declared so by the faculty on the day
of promotion to tenure. That this process is often rit-
ualistic is borne out by the countless tenured faculty
members who either cannot or will not teach and who will
go to any length to avoid the necessity of doing so.
Perhaps university administrations could counter this
deficiency in departmental management, but it is difficult. Why should an administration know more about the
teaching capacities of departmental members than the
department itself?

That students have complained and continue to com-
plain of unimaginative and indifferent teaching cannot
be attributed, however, to research-oriented universities and departmental leadership alone. For the level
of any individual's teaching reflects a personal decision. No university has a restriction against service
to students in all of its forms. If many faculty members have spent little time in improving their teaching,

redesigning their courses, or stimulating the intellectual life of the community, it is in some measure because they have found too little personal reward in doing so. Individual faculty members have moved comfortably into the mold created for them by the proclaimed emphasis on publication. Here the rewards have often been substantial. So why, believe many, waste time in teaching? Dexter Perkins analyzed this issue in his 1956 presidential address before the American Historical Association, "We have tended . . . to exalt the written over the spoken word in the practice of our profession. Both carry their special messages, but for most of us the possibility of reaching large audiences through what we write is not great. Our best chance of making impact on others will come through the influence we can exert in the classroom, through the enthusiasms we kindle, through the interests we arouse, through the wisdom that history teaches and that we can strive to disseminate. Here, as I see it, for all but the greatest and most imaginative scholar, is our greatest chance of usefulness, our largest hope."

Certainly historians and teachers in other disciplines have made no notable effort to follow Perkins' advice. Historians, like others, are employed to teach and, at least officially, that is their first obligation. The taxpayers and students expect no less. And many outside the classroom, who believe that they are paying for good teaching, simply assume that teaching is adequate and requires no special attention. The heavy enrollments of past years gave even the poorest teachers sufficient numbers of students and thus encouraged the complacency. If classes were overflowing, why should anyone except the students question the quality of instruction? Captive audiences can easily create illusions of success, and many of those audiences were captive. Now that enrollments are down and full classrooms are no longer automatic there is a new sense of urgency, a new spirit of competition. Distinctions become clearer. In recent years the historical profession has instituted a variety of means to improve teaching. This Newsletter has reported on new strategies employed by some history departments to attract students. Perhaps other disciplines are doing much the same. If they are more successful than we, our declining enrollments may well continue.

Such efforts, of course, have their limitations. Teaching is a private matter. It is an expression of personality--perhaps, even more so of character. Ultimately it comprises little but an influence. For that reason good teaching can be encouraged but, except at the most elementary levels, it cannot be taught. Most of us have had one or more superb teachers, but we really cannot duplicate their performances. The voice, the personality, the individual frames of reference do not permit it. I have had a number of excellent teachers during my undergraduate and graduate experience. Except for high levels of preparation, they had little relationship to one another, and I, liking them all, turned out to be far different from any of them. Ultimately my good teachers--especially Walter Johnson, Avery Craven, and Thomas Hutchinson at the University of Chicago-- could not tell me what to do. They could only establish standards as to what different styles of good teaching demanded.

Without good student response teaching has no chance; with good student response its possibilities for satisfaction and accomplishment are almost without limit. The challenge for any teacher is to gain that point of proficiency where classes become alive and student response sets in motion that rising spiral of intellectual and emotional interaction which ends in a totally satisfactory student-professor relationship. Students--and too few realize it--are an essential element in any successful classroom experience. Yet the initial responsibility for creating the necessary upward spiral rests with the instructor. Those who achieve it in varying degrees are generally known on any campus; those who do not are also known.

Much has been written and said about the importance of research to the development of good teaching. This assumption bears closer scrutiny. Many of the world's poorest teachers are brilliant scholars. There is simply no direct connection between good teaching and successful research. But it is equally true that research can contribute much to teaching. Clearly the broader one's research the more this will be true. Sometimes writing and research which focuses on many themes rather than on a few demands a professional price. Through the years I have written on a wide range of subjects. At times I have doubted the gains in all this effort. But, on the other hand, I seldom approach a topic in United States diplomatic history where my reliance is not almost entirely on my own writings--and writings, incidentally, which are not readily available to the students. It is this that produces originality, good organization and careful selection of materials, as well as a higher level of conviction. Here, perhaps, my opportunities have been unique. But the experience illustrates how research and writing contribute to the possibilities of good teaching.

Thus far I have distributed responsibility for improved teaching among university administrations, departmental procedures, and individual faculty members. Still there is a vital element missing from my evaluation of success in teaching. I have suggested that a college or university can have that for which it is willing to pay. Unfortunately, this is only partially true. If it were true, small colleges should have superb teaching, for teaching is the only responsibility of many small college faculty members. They are paid to teach, and that's it. But teaching is often no better at smaller institutions where the publish-or-perish syndrome does not exist at all. The reason for the almost universal failure of all faculties--college or university--to reach the level of possibility is because the necessary capabilities are not present. The best of writing, research, and teaching depends upon talents that are fundamentally rare. Universities have sought to encourage research and publication with special funding. They have spent hundreds of millions of dollars to achieve it. Yet these vast expenditures have, on balance, produced exceedingly limited results. Universities pay dearly for what they obtain. It may be that universities receive even less for their research dollars than they do for their expenditures for teaching. The ability to conduct meaningful research and obtain useful results belongs to the relatively few. And the ability to communicate well in writing is far more common than the ability to communicate through the spoken word, especially for periods as long as an hour. The talent to

14

speak clearly, logically, and persuasively day after day
is, in my experience, far rarer than the ability to
write good articles and monographs. During my quarter
century of teaching, happily at excellent universities,
I have had dozens of colleagues who have written excellent monographs. I have had far fewer who have made a
special mark in the classroom.

Many faculty members obviously have enormous talents for verbal communication but simply do not find the
rewards for teaching commensurate with the cost of preparation. To that extent there exists on every campus a
reservoir of potentially successful teachers for whom
university and departmental incentives for better performance could be highly significant. For most effective teachers, teaching has its own rewards, and they
are monumental. Some faculty members require special
encouragement to apprise them of that fact. But the
best teaching entails such an elusive combination of
personal attributes and receptive students that no university effort will produce universally satisfactory
results. Only in part can good teaching be purchased.

Universities exist to educate students. The challenge to mind and energy which students impose can be
stimulating beyond measure. To meet it, every teacher
must respond with a constant re-evaluation of performance and a determination to resist the pressures demanding selfishness. Because any course should be structured to deal with the material suggested by its title,
and not based on the personal and immediate interests of
the instructor, successful teaching requires a vast
amount of specific preparation which may, but usually
does not, deal with knowledge acquired from personal
research. There is no way to satisfy a teaching assignment on any occasion without careful preparation. Without such preparation a class often terminates in either
a rapid excuse for dismissal or a series of disconnected
comments without theme, substance, or validity.

Teaching is difficult and demanding; sometimes it
requires a measurable professional cost. But that cost
need not be exorbitant. There is time enough in the
career of those who so wish to teach and write effectively. If too few follow that course, be it for lack

of talent, energy, or incentive, there are still countless numbers who do. Their contributions lie at the
heart of the university endeavor.

II. INTRODUCING HISTORY TO COLLEGE STUDENTS

TEACHING HISTORY:
A CHANGING CLIENTELE AND AN AFFIRMATION OF GOALS

E. Bradford Burns

January 1983

Historians usually cite the 1970s as the decade of boom and bust for history teaching in colleges and universities. The hard times of the late seventies obscured memories of the heady expansions of the early years of that decade. A common consensus formed that the decade provided more problems than solutions. Yet, in deciphering the trends within the history department at the University of California, Los Angeles during those years, a notable and salutary pattern emerges. History courses are serving--and we hope are educating--an increasing number and greater variety of students than ever before. Without UCLA enacting any requirements, undergraduates are enrolling in more history courses in an apparent self-propelled search for breadth of knowledge. Happily, the department is achieving one of its major goals: to increase the young generations's perspective of the past in order to sharpen its understanding of the present.

This optimistic conclusion contrasts with some rather grim statistics. During the decade of the seventies the number of history majors at UCLA fell fifty-two percent; the number of graduate students dropped twenty-seven percent; and the number of permanent faculty members dwindled by twelve percent. Thus, if fall 1970 boasted 1,367 undergraduates, 384 graduate students, and seventy-two faculty members, ten years later those numbers were reduced to 650 majors, 270 graduate students, and sixty-five faculty. [The statistics for the Fall of 1984 closely resemble those of 1980. They reveal a slight rise in history majors (720) and permanent faculty (69) but a slight decline in the number of graduate students (255).]* These statistics, however, tell only one tale and not the most significant to my thinking.

Additional trends emerged during the 1970s [and

continued into the mid-1980s.]*   For example, statistics show that history course enrollments declined less
drastically than the number of undergraduate majors and
graduate students.   Classroom populations dropped only
eighteen percent between 1970 and 1980.   In fact, per-
centage declines in total enrollment and in the number
of permanent faculty members were approximate, suggest-
ing that perhaps fewer course offerings accounted for
the eighteen percent enrollment drop rather than de-
creasing student interest.   In any event, the significant point remains that courses offered in the 1980s
enrolled greater numbers of nonmajors, thus offsetting
the declining number of history majors.

My fall 1981 introductory class in Latin American
history illustrated the variety of student clientele.
One hundred fifty-three students responded to a query as
to their major.   Responses indicated twenty-five different majors in the social sciences, humanities, physical
sciences and life sciences, and from the fine arts and
engineering schools.   Another thirty-six, the largest
number of the sample, were "undeclared."   Only one out
of five was a history major.   [In May, 1985, I again
polled my introductory class to verify if the previous
variety remained.   The 121 students who responded represented twenty-seven different majors.   However, this
time one in three majored in history, and the number of
"undeclared" had dropped from approximately one in four
to one in ten.]*   A colleague who teaches a large
upper-division course in urban history has similarly
found that his course draws an equally varied student
population in which history majors are a distinct minority.

The rising student interest in history courses
resulted from no university pressures.   The College of
Letters and Science requires no history courses of its
18,000 undergraduates.   Students have a wide selection
of general and specialized courses within the social
sciences division, and they can graduate with majors in
humanities, social sciences, life or physical sciences
without ever attending a history lecture.   Of course,
some departments do specify one or another history
course for their majors, but even those requirements are
minimal.   Incontrovertibly, the increasing number of

students taking history courses reflects their willingness and desire to study the past.

Another related trend reveals that by the end of
the 1970s the lower-division program was attracting a
growing number of students. [During the Fall Quarter,
1984, for example, one undergraduate out of every nine
enrolled in lower-division history courses.]* Three
possible reasons explain the burgeoning enrollments.
First, freshmen and sophomores seem less concerned with
fulfilling requirements for a major and more open to
intellectual exploration. As a group, they are less
locked into a career track than their upper-division
counterparts. Second, the history department proudly
boasts that almost all the lower-division courses are
taught by experienced full professors with both distinguished academic and teaching records. Their reputa-
tions as stimulating teachers and scholars attract students. And third, the twenty lower-division courses are
general introductory courses, eschewing monographic
depth for broad significance. Three one-quarter courses
introduce students to the highlights of Western civilization. There are two series in United States history:
three one-quarter courses on the "History of the American Peoples" and two one-quarter courses on the
"Political History of the United States." Together the
history of science and the history of technology encom-
pass four courses. The remaining eight courses are
divided among introductions to Asian, African, Middle
Eastern, and Latin American histories. The broad perspective obviously attracts students who desire a general understanding of the past more than a specialization in a period, place, or people. The conclusion
seems obvious: the broader the course, the greater its
appeal to larger numbers of students. Conversely, as
specialization of topic increases, the appeal and thus
enrollment diminish. Here again some obvious exceptions
exist. "The United States since 1945," for example,
draws throngs of students to the classroom. Also, some
popular lecturers can count on an enrollment perhaps out
of proportion to the restricted historical topic in
their upper-division courses.

By their very structure, the lower-division courses speak directly and appealingly to Clio's new clien-

22

tele.   The students respond by enrolling.   I applaud
their decision.   They have a legitimate need for a broad
historical perspective.   Our professional duty is to
provide it.   Indeed, I believe that the students' search
for breadth may save the profession from its already
advanced state of fragmentation caused by overspecialization.   We might choose to ignore it, but the devilish
truth is that both fragmentation and overspecialization
have stultified the intellect of much of the profession.
Historians have increasing difficulty in fitting their
specialization into meaningful contexts and in making
those challenging comparisons and contrasts that require
the knowledge of several cultures and lengthy time periods.   Some of our colleagues are unable or unwilling to
teach survey courses. They lack the knowledge, vision,
ability, or a combination of the three.   Apparently, the
art of synthesis has become rare.   Our undergraduates
value that art.   They will be making increasing demands
on those who have mastered it.

The growing student clientele in search of a broad
introduction to history is the most positive trend to
emerge from the turbulent 1970s in the UCLA History
Department.   [That salutary trend continues through the
mid-1980s.]*   Others, of course, elect to dwell on
different trends.   As usual, statistics lend themselves
to a variety of interpretations.   Many lament the declining number of history majors and graduate students.
My own emphasis on the positive is not meant to ignore
budgetary realities or myriad other menaces.   Still, in
a period of despair, I simply suggest that all is not
lost. For while the crises of the 1970s reduced the
vigor of some history departments, those very difficulties have blessed us with new prospects. At UCLA at any
rate, the broadening appeal of history to greater numbers of students has pleased us.

In the final analysis, of course, much of the
health of the historical profession rests firmly in the
hands of the practitioners. We now look to the future,
a novel exercise since we spend so much of our time im-
mersed in the past. We surely will want to enhance the
status of our profession and to ensure the just position
of history departments.   I think we can do both.   Further, I think the means of doing so are rather obvious,

if not always easy. Let me suggest three.

First, we must learn to teach better. Our enthusiasms for the study of the past should be infectious.
We must constantly transfer our conviction of the significance and relevance of history to the young. Tedium
has no place in our lecture halls simply because no subject is more exciting than history. We must convey that
excitement.

Second, we must dispel some awful myths that not
only undermine the profession and teaching of history,
but also threaten the existence of the university as we
know it. These myths promote vocational training as a
logical part of the undergraduate curriculum in our
universities. Vocational training is needed; vocational
training is desirable; but vocational training has no
place in the curricula of undergraduate education of our
fine colleges and universities. The myths that I urge
we combat complement very subtly and insidiously the
concept of vocational training at the undergraduate level: namely that an economics major is the only portal
to business school; that a major in biology offers the
key to medical school; and that political science is the
logical springboard for a dive into law school. These
three erroneous stereotypes--and I could list others--
shape student mentality and perniciously influence
youthful academic planning. They pervert the meaning
and purpose of the university to the service of short-
term goals. Their ultimate impact on society is to create a vocationally competent population but, alas, an
uneducated one, a population ignorant of its past and
unprepared to meet the future.

The first critics of these myths, by the way, are
members of admissions and fellowship committees. Repeatedly they express their own annoyance with this
ubiquitous student mythology. Without exception, they
seek the unique, the well-rounded, the liberally educated student. Some fascinating studies indicate that
candidates for admission to a medical school who have
overly concentrated on science have lower rates of ac-
ceptance than those with a humanities or social science
major, assuming that the latter have taken some requi-
site science courses. On a most practical level, a

thought-provoking study from the University of California, Davis concerning students' chances of admission to
medical school reveals that a bachelor of arts rather
than a bachelor of science degree had a strong positive
impact on MCAT scores. Extra courses in humanities and
social sciences raised MCAT verbal and general information scores, thereby improving the odds of admission. At
one point, the report states, "An average white male who
took three or more courses in the basic humanities and
three fewer science courses would increase his probabil-
ity of admission by a staggering 39 percent."

Similar advice can be given to the legions of eager students who pursue a business career. For immediate and good employment, perhaps it is best to have a
degree in business administration, business education,
or economics, but for those who view themselves as the
future presidents or executive vice-presidents of hum-
ming industries, cashing paychecks of six figures, it is
more advisable to get a broad, general education. A
recent AT&T study noted that liberal arts graduates are
twice as likely as either business administration or
engineering graduates to reach middle- and upper-
management jobs in that corporation. Plenty of other
studies duplicate that conclusion. We can be grateful
that the professional world holds a liberal education in
high esteem. As partial thanks, we should communicate
their judgment to our undergraduates. We should also
point out that history better than any other discipline
furnishes the wide vision that thinking people and leadership require. Henry David Thoreau advised, "Read the
best books first or you may not have a chance to read
them at all." My paraphrase of that wisdom would be:
pursue the broadest education possible as an undergraduate because you will not have the opportunity to
achieve that breadth later.

Finally, it behooves historians to support curriculum reform. Indeed, most faculties are discussing
new core requirements these days. Such discussions offer an unparalleled opportunity for historians to exercise a powerful influence on the reshaping of higher
education. The propitious moment has arrived to abolish
or at least limit "irrelevant enrichment," that amazing
cornucopia of monographic courses prone to expand a wor-

thy detail into thirty tiresome lectures. Such courses rely on the students to fit the details into a meaningful context. Unfortunately, students lack the basic knowledge to validate that assumption. Countless studies reinforce what we know from classroom experience. The majority cannot identify Socrates, confuse the Enlightenment with the name of a rock band, and draw a blank when McCarthy, Kennedy, or Vietnam are mentioned. Somehow in the 1970s we reversed our priorities, abandoning the general courses, the surveys, to dwell on the details, few of which were ever woven into an intellectual fabric worthy to clothe our majors.

If we reduce the number of monographic courses, then it seems likely we can expand the number of survey courses. The good sense of the students will aid us in this task. Students want the general courses; we, the teachers, are best served by offering lively, meaningful survey courses. The energy, prestige, and the very best professors of our departments should be concentrated in those courses. Well-taught surveys should be the pride of the departments and their sustenance.

The termination of the ill-fated romance with the monographic courses and a return to the logical marriage to the general survey are the first step of curriculum reform. The next perhaps is more difficult and far more complex. Some of the curriculum reforms are exploring the interdisciplinary approach to learning, the challenging concept of crossing traditional departmental boundaries. That trend can benefit the profession. History logically and admirably serves as a nexus for interdisciplinary courses. In overseeing UCLA's honors collegium, a lower-division program dedicated to offering interdisciplinary courses to our best students, I long ago concluded that the majority of those courses depend heavily on history to provide the background and context for the subject under study. Through an active participation in interdisciplinary studies and a greater concentration on lively survey courses, history can play the major role in curriculum reform.

I am certain there are other steps we can take to ensure a healthy profession capable of playing a dynamic role in the academic future. I simply suggest we begin

with these three. Enthusiastic teaching, meaningful general courses, and a significant contribution to the new
core curricula will return to the historical profession
in the 1980s that academic leadership it lost in the
1970s.
----
        *Comments in the brackets are an update of the
column made by the author in May 1985.

History for Citizens

William H. McNeill

March 1976

College curricula used to give special place to history because it was assumed that study of the past somehow prepared one for life, imparting at least a possibility of wisdom or culture, or some combination of the two. In the past fifteen years, introductory history courses have generally lost special status as part of a required core curriculum. The odd thing is that historians did not usually resist the dismantlement of their curricular privileges very strongly--nor, of course, very effectively either. Teachers of general required courses had frequently lost faith in what they were teaching. Often they were beginners who felt that the best way to professional advancement was to teach their Ph.D. specialty and get out a first book as soon as possible. In the 1960s, when academic establishments were expanding more rapidly than our Ph.D. factories could equip budding academics with the professional union card, such a calculation was essentially correct. Few paused to ask whether the student public for courses in everyone's latest Ph.D. thesis was assured. General introductory courses were simply dismantled or made optional, whereupon students, reacting to the half-hearted way such courses were usually taught, took psychology, sociology or religion instead.

Our profession is now paying heavily for that rake's progress of the last decade. The study of history cannot expect to recover centrality in college curricula unless and until we have something to teach that speaks to general concerns of ordinary citizens. Specialized "post-hole" courses in subjects of arcane professional debate will not do. Their meaning depends on the pre-existence of opinions about the past to be tested and modified by precise investigation. But without a generalized picture of the past to alter, such courses float in a vacuum that makes them all but meaningless for ordinary students.

It is easy to say what introductory courses in history ought to try to do. Better than any other discipline, history can define shared, public identities-- national, civilizational, human as well as local, ethnic, sectarian. For obvious practical reasons, college courses must concentrate at the introductory level on shared identities. Familial, ethnic, class and sectarian histories that embrace only a small proportion of the students of any particular class have to take subordinate place. No doubt this tends to make historians conservative, emphasizing consensus and what is shared, while shying away from endorsement of divisive ideological definitions of the past. But smoothing over quarrels is not a bad thing; only if it is achieved at the expense of intellectual honesty can it be reprehensible.

What, then, are the public identities that matter most? Our national identity is central and inescapable; and national history remains relatively vigorous in our colleges for this reason. In the 1960s, disaster struck mainly in the extra-national field, when our profession's great artifact of the 1930s--Western Civ courses --collapsed. The fundamental idea behind such courses went something like this: Humanity has fumbled through the centuries towards truth and freedom as expressed in modern science and democracy, American style. Landmarks of the past that matter are those that contributed towards our contemporary pinnacle of skill, knowledge and wisdom. Meaningful history, in short, is the record of the progress of reason and liberty; and the place where it happened was Greece, Rome, western Europe and latterly the United States. An unspoken but very potent foil for such courses was the religious inheritance presumed in most students. The cutting edge of many a classroom lecture and discussion lay in an attack upon naively dogmatic religious formulations of the meaning of human history and life.

As the religious antagonist faded wraithlike from the minds of most students, the ethnocentrism implicit in such a view of the past became less and less convincing. One of the good reasons for the unravelling of Western Civilization courses was a growing recognition of the inadequacy of such an assumption. But so far historians seem to have found nothing to put in its place as an organizing principle for teaching general introductory courses. This failure is costly: unless we can find something else about the world beyond national borders that seems worth teaching to freshmen, the role of history in college curricula will continue to shrink.

An obvious alternative is to try to take on the world as a whole. Every day that passes makes it clearer that humanity is not striving unanimously to conform to American ideas of truth and freedom. Cultural pluralism and institutional diversity are far more evident than in the days when European empires extended over much of Asia and Africa. But amidst all the variety and confusion is there no principle that can focus attention and allow historians to find a meaningful pattern in the confusion?

This is the key question that ought to be before our profession in the coming decade. If we cannot reduce the unmanageable mass of potential information about the world's history to intelligible proportions, then our accustomed role of introducing students to their public identity as members of a larger society than that defined by national borders will wither away. Different and competing schemes ought to be devised, and new materials worked up for classroom use, as happened so successfully between 1925 and 1935, when the prototypes of later Western Civ courses were first constructed.

Intrinsically, the task of finding intelligible order in the history of the world is no different from what historians confront in making national or any other kind of history intelligible. Even the historian of a single city, labor union or university confronts potentially infinite source materials. Choices have to be made about what to leave out. Intelligible history is, in fact, a result of what we choose to disregard, just as all human communication is achieved by filtering out "background noise" from the confusing total sensory input available to us at any moment in time.

What is needed, therefore, is clear thinking about what is really important in defining public identities

and behavior in the world today. I, for one, believe
that heritages from the classical civilizations of Eur-
asia continue to define major aspects of human reaction
to the world. Heirs of ancient China, India, Islam and
Christendom remain fundamentally different from one
another; and an understanding of current events benefits
from knowing something about the ancient values and
institutions whose shadows linger, powerfully if often
subconsciously, still. Africa and Amerindian America
have less well defined, but no less powerful, cultural
inheritances from their respective pasts as well, that
ought also to be sampled in any satisfactory course in
world history.

Experiment can decide just how schematic our pres-
entation of leading ideas and institutions from these
ancient, classical pasts can and ought to be. Historians should be as able to find simplified but still useful definitions of what mattered about ancient and alien
cultures as we are to find useful labels and definitions
for periods or aspects of our national past.

Yet, to deserve the name, a course in world history ought also to take notice of key changes in patterns of interaction among the major cultures of the
earth. In recent centuries, the main benchmarks seem
clear enough. The opening of the world's oceans by
European seamen before and after 1500 is familiar and
obvious. Another general change came about 1850, when
old autonomies in most of Asia and Africa collapsed vis-
a-vis the western style of civilization. Perhaps 1950
will constitute a third such benchmark as the date which
non-western peoples again asserted their independence by
making wider use of technological and ideological de-
vices westerners had first brought to their attention as
instruments of imperial expansion.

For earlier ages the problem of constructing a
plausible world history is greater. I made one such
effort in The Rise of the West; other patterns can, perhaps, be generated if historians really try to find out
how best to present the history of the world to American
undergraduates. Yet so far, I must confess, there seems
remarkably little sign of any concerted, serious effort
to do so--or to find any intellectually satisfactory

substitute for the now discarded and largely discredited Western Civilization courses of the recent past.

This is ironic. Conditions in our profession are now ripe for constructive ventures, if the needful intellectual impetus can be generated. Few beginners will today reject a job on the grounds that they are not prepared to teach new materials. It follows that if deans, chairmen and senior professors can be persuaded that new introductory general courses are needed, and if our profession can generate a few viable models for such courses, a way opens for the study of history to reclaim some of the centrality it used to have in most undergraduate programs. New materials, new course structures, new adventures in the use of visual as well as printed sources will open up before us. A new generation of historians will be able to discover a message to offer the general college public, defining fundamental aspects of what it means to be human and thus heir to all the world's cultures.

If, on the contrary, such courses fail to appear, it is likely that historians concerned with matters outside the borders of the United States will follow classicists into academic limbo, where only a few abnormal students care to follow us as we explore details of our professional debates in the classroom. In such an event, students will look elsewhere for guides to living and for definitions of the collective, public identities that education inevitably does provide--if not through formal classroom experience, then informally through extra-curricular discussion and group behavior.

What historians do--and fail to do--in the next ten years should pretty well decide how things will go. It is high time to try something constructive: to think, experiment, persuade and prove to ourselves, as much as to others, that we still do have something real to say to ordinary students and citizens.

ADDENDUM--APRIL 1985

Very nearly ten years have elapsed since I gave the profession that much time to "decide how things will go." During that period, there have indeed been signs

of concern for new and better introductory courses in
history; and world history has become more nearly respectable as witnessed by the attention paid to programs
of the newly established World History Association at
AHA meetings.   But how successful efforts at creating
new introductory courses have been remains unclear.   So
far no one pattern or cluster of patterns for a new introductory course, either in United States history or in
global history, has made itself manifest in the way that
Western Civ courses did in the late 1930s before spreading across the country in the 1940s.

So the question remains unanswered.   History for
Citizens remains problematic to the profession.   We can,
however, take heart from the fact that decay of history
in the curriculum has been at least temporarily arrested
by a general move to return to basics and reaffirm the
importance of liberal education as against more immediately practical, job-oriented training in colleges. This
offers the profession a chance to regroup and decide
what it is that we ought to teach the young about the
history of their nation and of the world.   Until historians can agree on that, their reprieve from marginality
can only be temporary.

REFLECTIONS ON THE HISTORY OF WESTERN CIVILIZATION: AN UNBLUSHING APOLOGY, OR PERHAPS A LOVE LETTER

Evelyn Edson

February 1984

The possible demise of the Western Civilization course has been frequently discussed in the historical profession. As a teacher of Western Civ, I wonder if I am an endangered species on the way to extinction, having outlived my usefulness. Before being retrained, as a keypunch operator perhaps, I offer some reflections based on twenty years of teaching Western Civ.

I entered into the ranks of college Western Civ teachers at the University of Chicago, where I was a graduate student in the mid-1960s. A handful of us took a field rather rarely offered, I believe, in Western Civilization, taught by two masters of the art, Karl J. Weintraub and the late Christian W. Mackauer. We had to sit in on a section of the undergraduate Western Civ course and also take a seminar of our own choosing, reading such works as the Nichomachean Ethics, the Meditations of Marcus Aurelius, the historical philosophy of Kant, Hegel, Dilthey, and the like. We wrote papers, delivered them, and discussed such questions as: What is Western Civilization anyway? Where is it going? It was a wonderful program.

The next year, some few of us found a niche in the college Western Civ staff. At that time (1966), we were a large, disparate group of twenty to thirty teachers. We met from time to time to revise the readings, write the final comprehensive exam, and arrange for group reading of student papers.

The undergraduate course at Chicago at that time focused on carefully chosen primary source readings organized around selected historical problems. The readings were backed up by William McNeill's terse and to-the-point Handbook of the History of Western Civilization. We had three hours of discussion a week on the readings and a one-hour lecture on a special topic,

usually outside the students' reading (Mackauer on "The
World of Homer" or James Redfield on Book VIII of Thucydides, as examples). The first quarter of the course
dealt with Greece, Rome, and early Christianity. We read
Aristotle's Constitution of Athens, Thucydides, Plato's
Apology, and Crito, Sallust, Tacitus, the Gospel according to St. Matthew, some of St. Paul's letters, plus
various other short selections. Interpretive articles
by Weber, Rostovzeff, and others on the fall of Rome
were sometimes included, but not always. The second
quarter covered the Middle Ages through the Enlightenment, and the third quarter began with the French Revolution and ended about 1950. A heavy burden rested on
the student and the teacher to give these disparate
works meaning and unity. It was the work of the course.

Yet not every young teacher had come to the University of Chicago bent on teaching Western Civ. Most
considered the course an annoying distraction from their
real work, be it the study of the city of Nuremberg in
the 1650s or the Jansenist heresy in France, or the publication history of the Encyclopedia. Here true history
happened and was written. Western Civ was at best a
gross generalization, rather left to Arnold Toynbee. It
even pained one to speak in such grandiose terms as
"Renaissance" and "Middle Ages," or to make such irre-
sponsible comparisons as Augustine versus Abelard! The
young scholars at Chicago in those years were frankly
untrained in at least two out of the three quarters covered by the Western Civilization course. Hence, teachers often arranged to teach only their special section,
be it ancient, medieval-early modern, or modern history.

The course, however, had been originally designed
as a unit. I was most aware of this the year I taught a
summer session in which we swept through all of Western
Civilization in a breathtaking ten weeks. In this concentrated form, and with few other distractions, one got
to Mussolini, for example, before the students' vision
of Pericles had dimmed. It was marvelous, tracing the
many elaborate connections and comparisons that had been
built into the course.

In the hands of a master, such as Mackauer or
Weintraub, the course hung together wonderfully well,

and was one of the most respected and popular courses
offered in the general education program. Chicago's
graduates referred to it frequently as the course in
which they had learned the most, or which had been the
most stimulating. I can still see Mr. Mackauer gripping
the lectern, his white hair flying, and saying with his
customary intensity: "If at the end of this year you no
longer remember the date of the Battle of Salamis, I
will not care--although of course it would be better if
you did remember it. But if at the end of this year,
you are not a changed person, then I will be disap-
pointed."

As the course increasingly came to be taught in
three separate pieces by three separate specialists, its
unity could not fail to come unstuck. Students wondered
why they had to read Thucydides or City of God when it
was never mentioned again, except on the dreaded comprehensive. The great connections and interweavings and
intellectual leaps of the course were necessarily lost.
When I left Chicago, the course was in the process of
being fragmented. I hear it has since been revived. I
hope so, but I fear for its fate at a school like the
University of Chicago where teachers are expected to
publish specialized books in their fields. Not many of
us have the nerve to write in the field of Western Civilization.

But Western Civ continues to thrive out in the
boondocks, such as the community college where I teach.
Its rival is not World Civilization, as William McNeill
and others have proposed--at least not yet--but rather
American history. Here at Piedmont there are ten sections of American history offered for every three of
Western Civ, and they are bigger sections, too. Here,
Western Civ might be called "non-American history." A
non-American history course is not required in this
state's educational system after grade school. Most of
the students who take it take it out of a sense of
adventure. Their previous preparation in non-American
history is usually nothing more than an exposure to
classical mythology and a vague acquaintance with the
names of Julius Caesar, Marie Antoinette, and Napoleon.
My students' first reaction to the Iliad, their first
reading assignment of the year, is that it is full of

foreign names.

Now would it be better for these students to take
World Civilization, to put Lao Tse and Siddhartha alongside Achilles? Maybe, but I shudder at the thought of
the speed at which one would then sweep through not just
one, but all of the great civilizations of the world.
Perhaps if one could count on the students having had
some European history background from high school . . .
but one cannot count on that at all.

In teaching I have come to the conclusion that
less is more. Far better for the students to come to
grips with one early Flemish painter, than to have memo-
rized the names of a dozen.   Once long ago I taught a
group of students a unit on seventeenth-century political philosophy from a book that contained short selections from Hobbes, Locke, Filmer, and Harrington. Reading their exams, I was horrified to discover that a
number of them had hopelessly confused these four com-
batant gentlemen.   Now they read Locke alone, and a
great deal more of that. The mind boggles at four weeks
of China, four weeks of India, and its impact on the
ill-furnished mind.   To my practical teacher's mind
comes horrid visions of Krishna amalgamated with Kwan-
yin, of the Confucian code of the gentleman entangled
with dharma and the caste system, of Ulysses and Siddhartha in unholy alliance.

I think I would prefer a year of any single civilization as a history option rather than trying to fit
them all together in uneasy fellowship into a year's
course. So why focus on Western Civilization? For better or for worse our political system comes from England
and France, our religions from Jerusalem via Rome and
points north, our logic from Greece, our language from
Germany and England. We must live in the whole world,
but our perspective must come from a thorough grounding
in our own culture.

Gilbert Allardyce has shown us (American Historical Review, June 1982) that Western Civilization courses
are relics of outmoded World War I consciousness. Still
it is important to remember that to the students it is
all new. The tension between Athens and Jerusalem may

be a tired old concept to scholars, but to the students it is a new and exciting idea. The conflict between undying fame and the right hand not knowing what the left hand is doing, between "turn the other cheek" and sweet revenge, goes on right in their own heads. To consider the historical roots of such conflicts is intensely interesting. And one doesn't have to push Western Civilization as an intellectual imperialist in order to teach it. For example, consider the progress of reason and liberty. Who can stand in front of a classroom at this late date and argue for that? Instead one can introduce some of the dominant cultural themes, such as competitiveness, male dominance and female submissiveness, bipolar Western logic, and the Western attitude toward nature and technology. Students are astonished to learn that these are Western rather than universal human attributes. The last quarter of the course inevitably leads to the breakdown of Western confidence in the twentieth century. My students have just completed a final essay comparing the complacent attitude of the British in Forster's <u>Passage to India</u> with Hermann Hesse's <u>Siddhartha</u>.

In conclusion, I think there is still a place for the history of Western Civilization in our general education scheme and for general education in our college curriculum. My typical student comes from a nonacademic background. Many are the first in their families to go to college. Most of these students have never heard of many of the books we read. The course can open up to them an intellectual world that has formerly been closed. They frequently bring me magazine clippings or books to show me references to things we have just studied--see, here is Plato, here is Herodotus, here is Homer--as if to show me that they no longer believe I was making it all up. I think a college freshman in the 1980s needs to thrill to the trial and death of Socrates, the gentle blend of sanity and craziness in St. Francis, the dazzling array of intellectual building blocks of St. Thomas Aquinas. Then, after a hard, critical look at Western Civilization, they may be able to face the world.

ADDENDUM-MAY 1985

Discussing World vs. Western Civilization at the recent conference at Michigan State University ["What Americans Should Know," held April 21-23, 1985, at Michigan State University in East Lansing, Michigan] it became clear to me that we are not all talking about the same thing. Some Western Civilization courses are really European history, stressing events, causes, chronology, kings, wars and famous people. Others, like the Chicago course, are intellectual history, humanities or great ideas put into historical context. The World Civilization course, when it is not narrowed to topics or to a limited period, is a god's eye view of the movements of peoples, the rise and fall of empires, attaining an ultimate impersonality. Now there could be, and probably is, somewhere out there in American educationland, an interesting World Civilization great-ideas-in-context course, but to fit it into the academic year and include Western Civilization as well makes it either too superficial or too much. Since I teach a survey of Asia as well as Western Civilization, I know the amount of leading by the hand which is necessary to help students to understand works like The Analects or the Bhagavad Gita. How could it all be done in the time we have?

One answer is a two-year humanities sequence: one year for Western and one year for non-Western Civilization, taught in cooperation with other departments, such as literature and philosophy. But can we all claim so much territory? At the conference L. W. Spitz urged historians to become deans and grab the necessary turf.

Another possibility is to continue to teach Western civilization but with a slight World History twist, stressing influences, contrasts and comparisons--in other words, to put Western Civilization into a whole world context. This approach, while not so simple, does correct the Western chauvinist slant which is the basis for some criticism of the course.

The Western vs. World Civilization debate is not over. It can be a productive discussion for all of us, bringing up new ideas and challenging us to reorganize and rethink cherished courses.

THE SOCIAL FUNCTION OF HISTORY

Henry S. Bausum

September 1977

Taking history's social function seriously requires that history teachers give close attention both to <u>how</u> and to <u>what</u> they teach. Knowing how to teach has become of paramount importance because students' sensory perception frameworks have been dramatically altered in recent years. Knowing what to teach has become challenging because the structures of the history discipline and of society have each undergone pronounced and substantive revision in the past few decades. Current discussions on how to teach history can be viewed as one indication of a growing aim of historians to fulfill their social responsibilities. There is need for a comparable effort at defining what to teach secondary and college students in introductory history courses.

Some historians may believe that history fills a social need more responsibly today than it did a few decades ago when the old histories--Judaeo-Christian, national (at times racist), Whig, and some would include Western Civ--presented a limited and often biased view of the past. But rightly or wrongly, the old histories served a clear, even though dubious, social function since they described the rise and expected greatness of particular peoples and gave these peoples a sense of mission and purpose. They encouraged a belief in the superiority of Western values and culture, and reinforced the notion that a set of natural laws governed the affairs of men and of states. They not only provided a guide for conducting current affairs, they defined the grounds for viewing the future with optimism or hope. Although historians may view the ultimate collapse of traditional history and the emergence of a more authentic history as desirable and necessary, beginning students of history are often less impressed.

Since traditional history's collapse professional historians have been unable to agree on new and satisfying views of the past. To be sure the critique of the

old histories may have been an attraction to a past generation of students, but with that task effectively
accomplished some years ago, history has become increasingly meaningless to the general public. Historians
have found new bases for their own enthusiasm by broadening the chronological, geographical and social dimensions of history, but that enthusiasm has rarely been
transmitted to the introductory student--an exception
coming immediately to mind is women's history. We have
become a discipline of specialists. As a result, some
historians have given up all pretense at attempting to
introduce history to college students, sometimes justi-
fying their decision on the false assumption that most
of their students have already been introduced to history at the secondary level.

Historians have made a number of gestures toward
replacing traditional histories. Sometimes they have
undertaken these efforts with the primary intention of
developing courses for potential history majors. But
whether teaching history majors or the general student
public, distinguishing between what to include and what
to omit in an introductory history course is probably
the most difficult task confronting historians. It
should be clear, however, that the selection of details
is influenced, if not primarily determined, by the way
historians structure their accounts of the past and by
the organizing principles they adopt.

How do we respond to these difficulties when we
organize our introductory history courses? In spite of
theoretical arguments for a total history, historians
are often tempted to eliminate great portions of the
past by confining the chronological or geographical
scope of their introductory courses or by limiting the
dimensions of society's structure. Thus, the teachers
of many introductory histories have come to focus on a
more and more recent past. Others have shifted the
emphasis of their courses away from a study of the past
as such and have centered attention instead on historical methodology. This latter approach evolved gradually
over the course of several decades through collateral
books of readings for national and Western Civilization
courses. Some who were attracted to this approach ultimately gave up all pretense at introducing students to

the past and directed them to an examination of historical methodology as it applied to specific topics, sometimes the areas in which they were carrying on their own
research. Limited as these methods may be, they need
not signify a total dismissal of history's social function since a study of the recent past would seem to
inform students of their immediate origins and since a
study of historical methodology would seem to show students how to examine problems whether in past or present
society.

A more widespread tendency, one that historians
have often followed because it has proved popular with
students, has been to focus on narrowly defined topics.
The possibilities are so numerous as to seem infinite,
and although few teachers regard such topics as the history of women, revolution, or assassinations to be introductory histories, they are often a student's only
college course in history, and they are thus the sole
introduction to academic history which many students
ever receive at the college level. Valuable as such
courses may be in shedding light on specific aspects of
the past, they threaten to leave today's student with an
even narrower historical consciousness than that provided by the widely criticized political histories of
yesteryear.

One means of broadening the base of the topical
approach is to focus attention on five or six topics in
a single one-year course. The materials for such a program are admittedly not wholly satisfactory, and the
teacher who would develop it is faced not only with inadequate textual materials but with shortcomings in his
own understanding of widely disconnected aspects of the
past. This means of introducing history to students has
the advantage, however, of being flexible. It lends
itself to interdisciplinary treatment and to collabora-
tion with colleagues whose varied skills and interests
can be coordinated to compensate for individual weak-
nesses. A program developed along these lines at my own
institution has during each of the past five years sup-
plemented its discussion and teaching sessions with a
program of weekly lectures by guest speakers who have
represented virtually every discipline in academe. Yet
another way to take advantage of such popular topics may

be to incorporate them into a somewhat more traditional Western or World Civilization course through the "core-satellite" arrangement of the Kansas Plan. (See "Teaching History Today," October 1975.)

Equally important as structure in developing introductory programs is the adoption of principles or criteria for organizing material. In the case of topics or themes, separate organizing criteria might be necessary for each although some themes seem to reinforce one another. Whether the subject is as broad as world history or as narrow as a single theme, however, history's social function stands in greatest likelihood of being enhanced when organizing principles or criteria are carefully and consciously selected and used to determine what to include or exclude in the final introductory account of the past.

Perhaps the criteria for organizing introductory courses in history may emerge from present-day environmental concerns. Because the natural environment had an important bearing on the past, and will be an important determinant in the direction human society takes in the future, it offers the prospect of a new and attractive alternative to the traditional histories. By bringing humanity's long interaction with the physical environment under review, such course of study should help to reduce unwarranted alarmism and pessimism about environmental change and yet at the same time help to foster an awareness such as society--if it is to preserve its resources for the future--must acquire. Because the environment has a bearing on every aspect of life, and because our present attitudes and practices are deeply rooted in the past--in the record, among other things, of forests being cut, swamps drained, and virgin land plowed--the historian might have something to say about the environmental crisis as it relates to the present and the future, as well as the past history of mankind. Most of us assumed until recent years that the resources of the earth were inexhaustible; consequently, we have lacked valid criteria for making value judgments about human interaction with the environment. With the dawning awareness that human beings can exhaust in a few generations the resources of the earth and pollute the very air we breathe, it becomes clear that whatever is detrimental to the environment is also ultimately harmful to humanity. The history of human interaction with the environment, therefore, could help restore a sense of chronological meaning to a society that has become ever-increasingly attached to an illusive present. Some might argue that it is too early to write such a history. Still, a popular form of this history is already on the market and thus the question is simply whether society's sense of this aspect of the past will be formed by the popular press and media without the modifying and correcting influence of the historical profession in academe.

Other unifying principles also deserve our consideration or reconsideration because they may offer means for restoring vitality and social usefulness to national, Western and World histories. One such thought comes to mind from Montesquieu's concept of the need for a division of power among the executive, legislative and judicial branches of government. Is there a similar value in maintaining a division of power at the larger level among the economic, political and intellectual segments of society? To what extent, in other words, do societies become subject to totalitarian controls when the balance between the institutions of these parts of society break down? Are there, in fact, grounds for maintaining the need for a division of power within the economic and intellectual realms as well as the political? Does the past give any insight into the effect of such a balance or lack of balance on society?

The point of this discussion is that ideas of the magnitude suggested above deserve airing because historians are most likely to extend their insights into the workings of society and increase their social usefulness when they undertake to investigate the validity and applicability of such broad concepts. Thus, the Turner frontier thesis, with all its imperfections, has yet to find global application for introductory students. Toynbee's thesis of "challenge and response," whatever limitations we may find in his total work, might conceivably form part of the organizing basis for discussion at the introductory level. The place of power blocks and power vacuums in society, of social pressures for change and institutional recalcitrance to change, of the conflict

between society's need for order and the individual's
need for independence may not be fully understood by any
of us, and yet most of us would agree that some comprehension of the significance of these concepts aids in
comprehending both the past and present and will most
likely be equally important in lending insight to society's modus operandi in the future.

Organizing principles have often been set forward
as though they provided the single key to an understanding of history. When they have failed to do all we
expected of them, they have often lost their charm.
Perhaps we have expended too much energy in the past in
search for single keys and too little in exploring a
multiplicity of keys, each unlocking its own limited set
of doors. Perhaps we have directed too much of our critique of introductory histories toward ferreting out
minor inconsistencies and errors and too little toward
settling on the most plausibly authentic set of available explanations. This is not to suggest the need for
relaxing our critical skills, but to put historical criticism in proper perspective when it deals with broad
questions of interpretation for introductory students.

In short, a distinction between the needs as it
were of pure research and those relating to the application of knowledge to society's needs is important because academic disciplines must in final analysis serve
a social function if they can logically expect society
to be generous in the largess it grants them. History
no longer serves the social function which Leopold von
Ranke found so unsatisfactory. Were Ranke to look at
history's social function today, however, he might well
be less disturbed by the misuse than the nonuse of history and less by the transmission of traditional myths
to society than by the lack of communication between
professional historians and the members of society. In
a pluralistic society such as our own, no single history
may satisfy all of society's needs. Historians have it
within their power, however, to develop a plurality of
histories. To the extent that they can bring sense to
the past through these histories at the introductory
level, they should enlarge the social function of history and perhaps in the process begin to narrow the
presently existing gap between society's "two cultures."

III. HISTORY
AND THE
PUBLIC SCHOOLS

FROM HISTORY TO SOCIAL STUDIES

Lester D. Stephens

April 1977

A half-century ago most high school students were required to complete three years of history for graduation. Since 1913, however, when the term "social studies" was formally introduced in a preliminary report on the reorganization of secondary education, history requirements have been gradually reduced, and various social science courses have taken their place. Currently, history is simply included among many courses which are placed under the rubric of social studies in American high schools. The result is that history has lost some of its special identity while the social sciences have taken a larger place in the secondary school curriculum. In addition, the role of history has declined further as it has been integrated with other social studies. In fact, some educators go so far as to suggest that the study of history has limited value because it provides neither relevant knowledge nor useful generalizations on social and political behavior. Certainly, few of these proponents of a unified discipline of social studies want to abolish history study. But many of them do wish to make the study of the past a more "useful" subject, and they feel this can be best accomplished by making it more like the social sciences.

As noted by George H. Callcott in his History in the United States, 1800-1860, history found its way into the high school curriculum in the 1830s, and during the next three decades it became firmly established. Under the influence of Romantic ideas, history was viewed as "a pleasant and exciting subject of stirring narrative and intellectual adventure," and it was considered useful because it provided moral training, inspired patriotism, and improved mental discipline. After the Civil War, however, interest in the study of the past waned, and it was not vigorously revived until the late 1880s, when teachers and other public officials began to stress the contribution of history instruction to the formation of patriotic attitudes, cultural insights, and good citizenship. Although critical studies of the past took a back seat to idealistic history, the rising national- istic fervor of that era greatly aided the case for his- tory as a school subject. It was at this point that the American Historical Association began to involve itself in the reform of the secondary school history curricu- lum.

The first AHA committee on school history reform was appointed in 1896. Called the Committee of Seven, its membership included such illustrious historians as Andrew C. McLaughlin, Herbert Baxter Adams, Albert Bush- nell Hart, and Charles H. Haskins. The committee issued its report in 1898, and for two decades that report served as the authoritative guide on the secondary school history program. The committee claimed that the study of history would help to enlighten students about "the development of the human race," cultivate their judgments regarding the "relations between cause and effect," train them in the use of sources and evidence, and develop "the scientific habit of mind and thought." To achieve the fullest development of such worthy goals, then, the Committee of Seven recommended four years of historical study for high school youth, including one year each in ancient history, medieval and modern Eu- ropean history, English history, and American history and civil government. The committee's report also stressed the importance of sound pedagogical methods, calling for "a thorough and systematic course of study" that utilized original sources and provided continuity in syllabi and textbooks.

A few years later, the AHA appointed another com- mittee to study the teaching of history in elementary schools. Established in 1905, the Committee of Eight completed its report three years later. The committee suggested that a course in the "European Background of American History" be substituted for American history in the sixth grade, but it also recommended United States history for the fourth, fifth, seventh, and eighth grades. As noted by Rolla M. Tyron in his The Social Sciences as School Subjects, the impact of the commit- tee's report was small, and the only recommendation followed very widely at all was that for the sixth-grade history curriculum.

In 1907, the AHA appointed a Committee of Five to consider complaints about the overemphasis on ancient history in the report of the Committee of Seven. When it issued its own report in 1910, however, the Committee of Five largely reinforced the recommendations of the 1898 committee, but it did suggest that high schools devote more attention to the modern period in their history program. That recommendation was reiterated by the Committee on History and Education for Citizenship, appointed in 1918 by the AHA. Essentially, the report of this fourth AHA committee called for a twelve-year history program, of which the first three years would deal with the community and the next three with the history of the United States. After these two cycles had been completed, a third would commence in the junior high school, including studies of "the world before 1607" in the eighth, and "community and national activities" in the ninth. The last of these was designed to stress "recent economic and social history," combined with studies of "commercial geography and civics." Finally, the last cycle would include courses on "progress toward world democracy" for the tenth grade, "United States history during the national period" for the eleventh, and "social, economic, and political principles and problems" for the twelfth. Quite clearly, then, the recommendations of this committee reflected a number of larger forces at work, including the increasing influence of other professional organizations, new ideas on the role of the United States in international affairs, and changing views toward the necessity for including both non-traditional history and the social sciences in the school history program.

Meanwhile, both the American Political Science Association and the National Education Association were hard at work in efforts to reform the social studies curriculum. The first of these, the APSA, founded in 1903, became concerned when a survey indicated that university students were abysmally ignorant of certain basic facts about the American political system. Thus, in 1906, the association appointed a committee to study the teaching of civics in elementary and secondary schools. Issuing its report in 1908, that committee recommended an informal introduction to the fundamentals of government in the fifth grade, followed by a more detailed study in the eighth grade. Then, for the twelfth grade, the committee strongly urged a minimum of one-half year of study of government. This report seems to have resulted in little change, and thus the APSA appointed a follow-up committee, which completed its work in 1916.

Known as the Committee of Seven, this group recommended a year-long course in social science, of which one-half was to be devoted to the study of government. The committee also requested that colleges accept a full unit of social science for entrance requirements. In addition, the report contained an explicit statement regarding the development of good citizenship and increased attention to community affairs and the "machinery of government." Apparently dissatisfied with the implementation of the committee's recommendations, the APSA appointed the Committee on Civics Instruction in High School in 1920. That committee claimed that civics instruction was "spreading itself in unguided fashion" and that students were learning "a mere smattering of many things." Alarmed that the civics course now included "economics, sociology, ethics, and international relations," the committee deplored the extent to which the study of American government had been "thrust far into the background." Thus, while the APSA was concerned over the neglect of government at the expense of history instruction, it also viewed the willy-nilly rise of a conglomeration of social studies with disfavor.

An even more significant influence was spreading in the meantime under the sponsorship of the National Education Association. Concerned with developing good citizenship in the schools, the NEA appointed the Committee of Ten in 1892 to study ways to achieve its goal. A special division of the committee functioned as the Conference on History, Civil Government, and Political Economy. Among its recommendations were a minimum of eight years of history, an emphasis on biography and mythology, studies in civil government, and instruction in commercial geography and economics. The NEA followed up, in 1893 and 1895, with other committee studies, but the greatest impact from that organization was not felt until after World War I.

In 1913, the NEA established a Commission on the

Reorganization of Education, which consisted of seventeen committees. Among them was the Committee on Social Studies, whose recommendations were ultimately to have far-reaching effects upon the role of history in the secondary school curriculum. In summary, the committee's report in 1916 called for courses in European history for the ninth and tenth grades, an American history course for the eleventh, and a "Problems of American Democracy" course for the senior year. Obviously, history was still considered important, but its scope had been reduced. The committee devoted appreciable attention to the "problems" course, declaring that civics courses were inadequate as currently constituted and that they neither "met the needs of high school pupils nor satisfied the demands of economists and sociologists." In addition, the committee defended the teaching of other "social studies" in the junior high school years. It was at this point that the term "social studies" began to gain vogue, and ultimately, of course, it took precedence over the older terms used to designate the separate disciplines it embraced.

Under such influences as the NEA's report, changing ideas on the content of historical study (as advocated by James Harvey Robinson and other historians), increasing development of the social sciences, and reinforced demands for training good citizens, the social studies experienced phenomenal growth. The AHA could not ignore this trend, and it again became involved in studies of the school curriculum. Thus, in 1919, it appointed the Committee on History and Education for Citizenship, but the committee's recommendations for including eight years of historical study (from the third through the eleventh grades) found no favor among social scientists who rightly concluded that their subjects had been largely ignored. Finally, the AHA agreed to cooperate with social scientists on the matter, and in 1926, the Commission on the Social Studies in the Schools was established. The membership of this commission included many accomplished historians and social scientists, and the efforts of the group were indeed prodigious. In the final analysis, however, the commission's reports were largely ineffective, for as Erling M. Hunt has observed, that body "failed to discharge its most important responsibility," that is, to determine the content of courses designed to attain the stated objectives of instruction in the social studies. But, as Hunt also notes, the commission did make "social studies" a respectable term, and it concurred with the idea that social studies instruction was essential to the development of responsible citizenship. Thus, even the AHA had in effect conceded that school history was now one of the social studies and that its role was to be viewed as "useful" to citizenship training rather than as a liberal study.

While all of this was transpiring, efforts were under way to integrate or "fuse" history with the other social studies. It was first begun in earnest by Harold Rugg and other followers of John Dewey's ideas on education, but it continues into the present. Although these efforts have generally failed, there are still a number of educators who feel that history's role ought to be further subordinated because, as one recent methods textbook on the social studies claims, history deals too much with the unique and too little with "regularities in human conduct." Moreover, the same book declares that history and the social sciences still "compartmentalize knowledge and methods of investigation which relate to the study of man." It is that very idea which lies at the heart of the controversy over the place of history in social studies instruction.

To be sure, many historians recognize the important contribution of the social sciences to historical inquiry, and some historians have published significant studies utilizing social science concepts and methods. But the net effect of the efforts of those who would completely integrate history with other social studies has been a loss of the sense of the importance of history as a unique kind of knowledge about man and his social relations as well as utter confusion over the content of the social studies in general. What some of the greatest thinkers of our own time have been unable to accomplish in terms of unifying all knowledge of a social nature, some educators have nevertheless persisted in advocating. To criticize their efforts, however, is not to suggest that we restore history to the dominant role it played in 1900. It is instead a criticism of their failure to recognize that there are many dif-

ferent ways to study the animal called man and that history makes its own significant contribution to that
goal. History, properly taught, is a liberating study.
It certainly cannot do the job alone, for other forms of
social inquiry are also essential. But history could
stand a revival of its identity as a distinct type of
study beneficial to every secondary school student.

The key to improving the role of history instruction in the secondary school lies not so much with history's place among the social studies as it does with
how well the subject is taught. The controversy over
history and the social studies has arisen mainly over
the question of whether history should be just like any
of the other social studies. When it is viewed as a
critical and informative study of human activity in a
social setting, however, history is a unique type of
inquiry. What we need, therefore, are more teachers who
have been thoroughly trained as historians and who are
allowed to concentrate upon the particular contributions
of the study of the past to our understanding of the
present. Certainly, such teachers must be exposed to
those social sciences which enlarge their understanding
of social and political behavior, just as teachers of
the other social studies must be adequately trained in
their respective social science disciplines. But neither the history teacher nor the social science teacher
should be expected to serve as masters of each other's
disciplines. Although this is a somewhat idealistic
view in light of current certification requirements and
established notions prevalent in the whole process of
training teachers, it is nevertheless important if we
are to restore history to its proper place in educating
our youth. As historians we can be content with letting
history remain in the category of social studies if we
can secure a better understanding of its special role.
It is to be hoped that recent efforts of professional
historical organizations to improve the quality of history instruction will bring about the desired results.

ADDENDUM--MAY 1985

Several years ago I directed a course on methods
of teaching the social studies and supervised student
teachers in the same area. I also was a consultant to

many secondary school programs in the social studies.
Gradually I came to the conclusion that many teachers
were not prepared adequately to teach history or other
subjects in the social studies. My thoughts on these
problems ultimately led me to investigate how the discipline of history had lost some of its special status in
the schools. At the same time I wished to make a case
for renewal of its unique place in the curriculum. The
result was the column, "From History to the Social Studies."

Since I published the column, many state and national leaders in education have articulated their concern over the inadequacies of secondary-school curricula. Among their concerns is the failure of school and
college history programs to prepare students well in
understanding U.S., western, and non-western cultures
and their historical development. I share this concern,
and I continue to believe that in part we are not doing
a good job because we are falling short in developing a
historical sense. I maintain that colleges must train
prospective history teachers more thoroughly by requiring them to major in history and to complete a course
that deals with the nature of historical inquiry. The
latter must include an examination of historical sources
and evidence, a consideration of the problems of objectivity, bias, and evaluation in the writing of history,
some substantial research projects that draw upon primary sources, and considerable practice in historical
writing.

Since I wrote the column, the peak of advocacy for
integration of history with the other social studies has
largely passed, a view which seems to be sustained by
the excellent report History in the Schools, edited by
Matthew T. Downey and published in 1985 by the National
Council for the Social Studies Special Interest Group
for History Teachers. Thus, historians can now focus
more attention upon the proper preparation of secondary
school history teachers and upon the history curriculum
itself. Still, it is useful to remember how the role
and place of history in the schools have changed since
the turn of the present century.

IV. TECHNIQUES IN TEACHING HISTORY

FILM STUDY AND THE HISTORY CLASSROOM

John E. O'Connor

March 1977

Since 1895, when Auguste and Louis Lumiere put on the first public exhibitions of moving pictures, hundreds of thousands of films have been produced. The movies that survive as testament to that eighty-two year history of an art form--documentaries, theatrical features, serials, newsreels, propaganda films, training films, television commercials, and more--represent a tremendous storehouse of raw material for the history classroom. Each film is a historical artifact, a unique document for classroom analysis, and an effective tool for motivating students to consider all sorts of historical questions.

Perhaps the most productive approach to the use of film in the history class is to treat it as one would any other historical document. This requires that the teacher immerse himself to some degree in the study of film language and film art--something for which graduate school prepares very few historians. But the effort expended in learning to deal knowledgeably with film can yield significant results. Bringing film documents to students serves three principal purposes: (1) to give them practical experience in historical analysis and logical thinking, (2) to motivate them to study more traditional historical problems, and (3) to increase their awareness of the film experience by teaching them some of the basic elements of visual communications. This third purpose is based upon the premise that most of today's so-called "media-minded" young people do not comprehend even the first principles of how film and television communicate. Although some disciples of Marshall McLuhan will disagree, spending so many passive hours in front of the TV has lulled most viewers into suspending judgment and allowing themselves to be swept away into a sort of dream world. Rather than fine-tuning their analytical skills, they allow themselves to be hypnotized before the screen, taking in its messages uncritically.

58

Despite the belief of some teachers that showing a
film in class represents a capitulation, an admission
that the Gutenberg era really is dead, nothing could be
further from the truth. What it does indicate is a re-
alization that students are attracted to film and a belief that this interest can somehow be transferred to
their study of history. Equally important, it suggests
an awareness of the teacher's responsibility to help
students develop the analytical skills necessary to seek
out information, to verify it, and to evaluate it critically. Like most Americans today, students of the 1970s
receive their everyday information more from the six
o'clock news than from books, newspapers, or magazines.
To close our eyes to this phenomenon would be the real
capitulation. Reading comprehension is as important as
ever, but teaching an understanding of visual perception
and inculcating the skills of visual comprehension merit
our attention as well.

Documentary films are of more obvious value as
historical artifacts than theatrical feature films.
Usually there is more to be learned from the "actuality"
footage of a documentary than from the costumes and sets
designed in a Hollywood studio. Naive to lens and
lighting techniques and the tricks of editing, students
at first may feel that they are seeing the actual historical events happen before their eyes. Discrimination
takes place as the teacher asks searching questions and
challenges students to look again. In the process students should develop a capacity for heightened visual
awareness, and they may find themselves fascinated by
historical questions that perhaps seem meaningless and
dull when approached through a lecture or a textbook.

Two documentaries I have used to good effect are
The Plow That Broke the Plains, produced by Pare Lorentz
for the United States Resettlement Administration in
1936, and See It Now: Report on Senator McCarthy, Edward R. Murrow's expose of Joseph McCarthy aired by CBS
in March 1954. Each running about thirty minutes, these
films are readily available, convenient to use, and
quite inexpensive. What makes them especially interesting examples is that in at least some small way, in
addition to illustrating historical developments, they

helped to shape them.*

A pertinent question to be asked about any historical document concerns its authorship. The Plow That Broke the Plains was made under the auspices of the United States government. Its purpose, as spelled out in the official records of the sponsoring agency, was to publicize the activities of the Resettlement Administration, the agency responsible for finding new homes for families forced off their farms by the environmental calamities of the middle thirties. The film purports to tell the true story of the Great Plains by tracing its settlement, first by cattlemen in the 1880s and then by hardy homesteaders who could find no vacant land elsewhere. They suffered in the semiarid climate where cyclical dry spells withered their crops, but they survived until World War I when soaring grain prices tempted farmers and unscrupulous land companies to overexpand production in marginally tillable lands. During the war and in the early twenties they plowed the plains so extensively that the next time drought came there was no grass to hold the soil, and it blew away. The closing sequences of the film show caravans of migrants, made homeless by the swirling dust, joining "the great army of the highway," looking for "a chance to start over." The implication was clear. The Democratic administration in Washington was sensitive to their plight and the Resettlement Administration was meant to help them.

The next logical question about a document refers to its audience; who saw the film and how did they react to it? Although film critics voiced acclaim, The Plow That Broke the Plains became the focus of a controversy between the administration in Washington and Hollywood producers who feared government competition in the movie business--similar to the power companies' reaction to the T.V.A.--and who responded by discouraging commercial exhibitors from booking the film. Democratic politicians liked the movie, and several incumbents used it to impress voters in their 1938 bids for reelection to Congress. Republicans correctly perceived it as propaganda for F.D.R. and his New Deal program. But the most serious criticism came from inside the Resettlement Administration itself, from agents stationed in still fertile sections of the Great Plains where dust storms had been

no problem. They charged that the film misrepresented
conditions by generalizing about the area, and ultimately their arguments served to support Republican
efforts to have the film withdrawn from circulation.

By the time all this has been brought out in
class, perhaps discovered by the students themselves as
they study memoranda reprinted in Richard D. MacCann's
The Peoples' Films: A Political History of U.S. Government Motion Pictures (New York, 1973), they should be
anxious to reevaluate their first impressions of the
film. If time permits it might be screened again, or a
sequence-by-sequence outline of the film might be prepared for class discussion. My own mimeographed outline
of this film, describing visual and oral components in
side-by-side columns, runs to five pages.

Since The Plow That Broke the Plains is free of
copyright restrictions, it is possible to videotape sequences or make 35mm slides of single frames for discussion by the class. The photography of the film is ex-
quisite; many shots resemble the depression photo studies of Walker Evans and Dorothea Lange. The symbols and
transitions (sledge hammers on fenceposts, newspaper
headlines superimposed on whirring presses, phalanxes of
tanks and tractors choreographed to World War I music)
may appear clumsy and old-fashioned to a generation so
overexposed to the technical skills of modern television, but this very characteristic makes them easier for
film-study novices to identify and analyze.

Detailed structural analysis reveals more as significant historical questions emerge directly from the
visual context of the film. For example, the 1920s are
presented in a montage of belching smokestacks, overflowing grain hoppers, a jazz drummer, and a stockticker
which teeters for a minute on its platform before crash-
ing to the floor. Then the film cuts directly to the
thirties, the depression, and the dust bowl. The visual
implication (post hoc ergo propter hoc) is that the
crash caused all the trouble. The opportunities for
classroom research and study projects leap from the
screen: What were the farmers' problems in the twenties
and thirties? Did they start before or after 1929?
What, if anything, did the stock market have to do with

them? What other sorts of images might have been chosen to portray the twenties? What were the real causes of the Great Depression and how did it affect urban and rural America differently? More generally, teachers might ask students to find out whether the pattern of western migration shown in the film was typical and challenge them to illustrate it with other non-film materials. They might also be prompted to consider the impact of inventions such as barbed wire and motorized farm machinery on the land and the people.

Equally effective in raising issues is Edward R. Murrow's See It Now: Report on Senator McCarthy. Most students have a vague conception of what McCarthyism means, but they have never seen more than a textbook photo of the man himself, and viewing the film brings him to life for them. There is considerable background information available about the production in Fred W. Friendly's book, Due to Circumstances Beyond Our Control (New York, 1966). Here again, substantive historical questions emerge directly from the visual fabric of the film.

A sequence-by-sequence review quickly reveals how it was organized--first showing statements by McCarthy and then showing him contradicting himself. The film is filled with examples of the senator's tactics that shock even today, such as his reference to candidate Stevenson in 1952 as "Alger, I mean Adlai" and his badgering of State Department official Reed Harris before his Senate committee. But in the process of putting together the film clips to show the senator in the worst possible light, Murrow seems to have fallen into some of the same techniques used by the man he was exposing. Sections of McCarthy's speeches were taken out of context, and certain sequences appear to have been included more because of the expression on the senator's face or the tone of his voice--at one point a silly little laugh makes him appear to be insane--rather than the substance of what he had to say. Other sequences--his response to a testimonial dinner, for example, where he sputters and shuffles his feet for a minute or two before admitting to be speechless--seem to have been included primarily to embarrass McCarthy. They tell us nothing of the methods he used or of the real dangers his movement

represented. The fact that the film has been credited
with helping to turn public opinion against the senator
just a few weeks before the commencement of the Army-
McCarthy hearings makes it all the more interesting. The
film can become the center of an entire unit on McCarthy
and the fifties and in the process help to sensitize
students to the techniques of communicating visually.

There is a place in the classroom for almost every
kind of film document. As those who rummage about in
the ruins of ancient civilizations discover immediately,
some artifacts are inherently more valuable than others.
But it almost always depends on the questions one is
asking. Dramatized feature films may be of little value
in studying traditional political or military history,
but if the framework of a teaching unit is shifted
slightly they too can become useful. The famous Odessa
steps sequence from Sergei Eisenstein's Potemkin, for
example, is fabricated history--it never actually happened. But the film provides dramatic insight into what
the Soviet government which sponsored the film wanted
its people to think and feel about the czar and his
troops. In addition, it is a beautiful example of the
way in which a film maker can translate political emo-
tions onto a moving strip of celluloid. The motives of
Hollywood producers over the years have had far more to
do with profits than propaganda, but the productions of
their "dream factory" can be at least as valuable as the
novels of a given period for helping the students to
develop a feeling for the time. Here again, historians
should take care to preserve the integrity of the film
as a work of art. They should encourage their students
to consider the background of production and audience
response, and study the film's visual context as well as
its surface subject matter. In short, film deserves the
same attention as you would give to any other historical
document.

Rather than simply generalize, I have gone into
detail about specific films here to accentuate the special values of film study to the history teacher. To be
sure, this is only one approach; educational films designed specifically for history classes can be useful
too. But teachers should become more aware of the vast
stockpile of visual historical documents available for

classroom use. They can help teachers generate interest
in history while at the same time serving to train students and teachers alike to comprehend more fully the
popular media of the present.

*The Plow That Broke the Plains can be rented inexpen-
sively from many commercial film outlets or it may be
purchased from the National Audiovisual Center, Washington, DC 20409, for about $70 (now $180). See It Now:
Report on McCarthy is available for three-day rental at
$20 from the CBS Publishing Group, 600 Third Ave., New
York, NY 10016. For further reading on film history and
analysis and their applications to the classroom see
Teaching History With Film by John E. O'Connor and Martin A. Jackson, pamphlet #2 in the AHA series "Discussions on Teaching." The bibliographies and lists of
film distributors printed there merit attention.

ADDENDUM--July 1985

At this writing, the version being sold of The
Plow That Broke the Plains still does not include the
epilog which was appended to the film in the original
release. The epilog can be viewed at, or purchased in
videotape copy from, the Audiovisual Division of the National Archives.

In 1985, perhaps even more than in 1977, history
educators need to be reminded about their responsibility
to train students in the skills that will be required of
them as active citizens in a participatory democracy.
Twenty years ago this meant teaching them to read the
newspaper critically and to distinguish fact from opinion as published there. Today it requires us to give
them the tools of critical viewing, what some have
termed "visual literacy." A current AHA project, funded
by the National Endowment for the Humanities, is developing classroom approaches to media materials as documents or artifacts. The results of this project will be
published in 1986. Meanwhile, those interested in the
use of visual sources in research and teaching would do
well to study the pages of the journal, Film and History, published quarterly from New Jersey Institute of
Technology (Newark, New Jersey 07102) by the Historian's
Film Committee, an affiliated society of the AHA.

USING PRIMARY SOURCES IN TEACHING SOCIAL HISTORY

Patricia Ebrey

November 1980

Many historians use primary sources as assigned readings in their courses. In certain areas, especially intellectual history, selecting texts and deciding how to approach them pose no unusual problems. But this is not the case with social history. Much of modern social history is based on quantitative sources which do not make for lively reading. Other sources such as wills, deeds, and contracts often seem too fragmentary or too technical to be analyzed by beginners. Therefore, to fill the gap, teachers often assign texts which they hope will give students a "feeling" for life in the past, short stories, diaries, and travelers' descriptions.

However, this approach also has defects. To present primary sources as adjuncts to the heart of a course, as mere illustrations of the conclusions drawn from other evidence, deprives students of the chance to try their own hands at historical analysis. Moreover, it is often difficult to organize a coherent discussion around these sources. Almost any story, description, or personal account contains information or insights on such a wide range of subjects that students tend to jump from one topic to another. As a result, many teachers who assign these types of readings never discuss them in class. But without guidance students often draw erroneous conclusions from what they have read, thus defeating the purpose of the assignment.

Much of my time during the past four years has been spent compiling non-quantitative materials for a sourcebook for Chinese civilization and social history. In the process I developed some notions about how to use primary sources in teaching social history and, I think, these may be of interest to other history teachers.

My sourcebook began as an effort to enliven the teaching of Chinese history by introducing texts which would show how individual people saw their world--the view from the bottom, if you will--rather than the overall scheme or view from the top. I wanted to find selections that would illuminate Chinese ways of thinking and acting in such areas as popular religion, family life, village organization, and social relations. As an historian, I had always been attracted to the local, the particular, and the personal. Anecdotes, epitaphs, letters, and short stories remained vivid in my mind and I repeatedly recalled them when I was investigating some aspect of the Chinese social system. Although I would have admitted that these sources could seldom be used to establish facts, I became convinced that they provided excellent teaching material.

Thus, with the support of the National Endowment for the Humanities and the help of several assistants and collaborators, I collected, translated, and tested in class about two hundred selections. Less than half of them ended up in the final book. Some were excluded because they failed to arouse student interest. But many more were rejected because my conceptions of the classroom uses of primary sources changed as I organized classes around groups of readings and as I wrote introductions. I continually returned to the question of what students were supposed to be learning from these primary sources.

Students, in discussion or in written evaluations, would say that they "enjoyed reading" a selection or "learned a lot" from it. But what had they actually learned? Almost all of them made basic errors in interpretation. They confused ideals and expectations, opinions and facts, and one person's perception of another for that person's perception of himself. To give an example, after reading the "Classic of Filial Piety" or "Stories of Admirable Women," students would launch discussions about how a society could operate with strongly ingrained attitudes of obedience and loyalty from subordinates to superiors. They assumed that because I had assigned a reading it had to be "true" and did not stop to question whether ideals could be genuinely held but not be a description of behavior. Or if they read an essay complaining of the flattery and corruption of men in high places, students quickly concluded that what the author said was objectively accurate and used the essay to discuss the operation of the central government rather than the attitudes or feelings of a certain person in a particular time and place. Or if I assigned a play or tale, most students took for granted that it was to be used as a "realistic" portrayal of how people acted, apparently not pausing to reflect that what entertained or inspired or fascinated people was by no means the same as what they thought and did in daily life.

In class I found myself repeatedly cautioning against what selections could not say and providing suggestions about the kinds of information they did offer. Pressed to defend my selection of pieces--I could not place the blame on some anonymous editor--I had to develop criteria for evaluation. Clearly the sources differed and had to be judged by different standards. In working out such standards, I found it necessary to divide my sources into four categories: personal accounts, descriptions, agreements, and cultural documents. These categories proved useful not only to my editing but also to my teaching.

In personal accounts an identifiable author discusses his own situation or expresses his own views. At their best such authors can provide as reliable evidence as the "native informants" of anthropologists. Examples of personal accounts in my sourcebook include letters, diaries, essays, and autobiographical sketches. Pieces were chosen because the authors were especially successful in articulating their thoughts and observations. In introducing personal accounts, I try to instill a few questions in students' minds: How does the author see his world? Does he think other people disagree with his views or act on contrary principles? If his point eludes us or seems illogical, could he be making an assumption we ordinarily do not make? Analyzed in such ways, personal accounts provide excellent testimony about the conceptions and mental habits by which the author and his peers oriented their social behavior. However, there is a danger in relying too much on such accounts: we might see only the culture of the highly educated who left written records. In a complex society such as China, with considerable differentiation according to class, sex, occupation, and region, the culture

of the literati was in many ways distinct from that of
other parts of society; one must guard against assuming
that the lives of scholars and peasants were based on
identical principles.

The sources I had collected to show the ways of
thinking and acting of ordinary people fell into three
categories. The kind most familiar to both students and
teachers are descriptions, that is, outsiders' observations. These include educated men's descriptions of the
lives, thoughts, and activities of women, peasants,
workers, rebels, and so on. Examples in my book were an
official's report of abuse of workers, a chronicler's
account of minority groups, and an essayist's description of rural folk. The standards by which such works
should be judged are the objectivity and sensitivity of
the observer. Is a description useful mainly because
the author reveals the prejudices that members of the
group he described had to cope with? Or does he de-
scribe the viewpoint of members of the group much in the
way they would have described it themselves? In compiling my sourcebook I discarded many descriptions because
I decided I could place too little reliance on the observer. Yet when dealing in class with the descriptions
I retained, I still found that questions of objectivity
and sensitivity were useful ones to raise in initiating
a discussion.

Agreements, such as tenancy contracts, mortgage
deeds, marriage contracts, lineage rules, and village
ordinances, often can reveal more about the lives of
ordinary people than descriptions. Even if the basic
outline of an adoption contract or a property division
deed was copied from a standard manual, its wording was
of great importance to particular individuals; its pro-
visions shaped the activities and the opportunities of
those who signed it, especially the weaker party. This
is true of almost any agreement, but for teaching purposes the more typical ones are probably most useful.
Because agreements are short, students often fail to
recognize their rich content. Yet the shortness of
agreements also makes them perfect for detailed analysis
in class, where students can be asked to reread them and
point out each of the principles underlying the social
and economic relations between the parties.

The final type of source valuable for probing the world of those who did not write I term "cultural documents." These are documents that transmit the thoughts, assumptions, and values which make up culture. Included are popular moral primers, folktales, novels, guidebooks to good manners, newspaper articles, and so on. These works are important for what they communicated to the audience which responded to them and kept them in circulation. The most popular ones can be assumed to have had the greatest impact and therefore are most deserving of analysis. Although it was not difficult to select good examples of cultural documents, it was difficult to advise students how to interpret them. One problem was that many of them are useful not for their literal content but for their symbols; we should search for meaning in them in much the way anthropologists find meaning in rituals, folktales, and myths. This requires greater imagination on the part of both students and teachers, and indeed is more an art than a science. But it is also a highly promising means of gaining access to what was going on in the minds of ordinary people.

To give an example, two of the most widely read Chinese novels are the Water Margin and Chin Ping Mei, one about a band of outlaws and the other a polygamous household and a woman of unexcelled spitefulness and cunning within it. Should we read these novels to learn about outlaws or concubines? They certainly were not the authors and must have been an insignificant proportion of the audience. The novels undoubtedly contain realistic details, but that is not why ordinary people loved to read them or see incidents from them performed on stage. To make full use of these novels as sources for social and cultural history, we must look at them as mythology, as conveyors of powerful symbols, whose importance was all the greater because of their exaggeration and distance from everyday life. For instance, could it be that outlaws, by breaking the rules of conduct, demonstrated (in an entertaining way) precisely what those rules were? Could it be that basic conceptions of power and subordination were conveyed by the contrast between the docility and fearfulness of the peasants and the courage and cruelty of the outlaws? What about the contrast between the docility and fearfulness of the peasants and the courage and cruelty of

70

the outlaws? What about the contrast between the outlaws and the equally outrageous, but seldom as good-
hearted, officials?

This analysis of the kinds of non-quantitative
primary sources useful for teaching social history influenced the direction of my scholarly work. But more
pertinent here, it enabled me to provide a clear direction to classroom discussions of translated primary
sources. Students today have often had considerable
introduction to methodology in their social science or
natural science courses, and I found that most of them
readily recognized that methodology is also crucial to
history. They could see that statements about traditional Chinese popular morality had to be based on surviving texts, and that how one could draw those inferences was as important and interesting a question as
what those inferences were. Of course, most of class
time was still devoted to questions of substance: how
were Chinese villages organized, what role did educational practices play in shaping upper class attitudes,
and so on. But linking these diverse discussions was
the issue of how we could know, from surviving sources,
anything about these questions. Students could compare
the generalizations they read in textbooks and scholarly
articles to what they could infer from primary sources,
and were often quite willing to suggest that the "au-
thorities" might have arrived at their conclusions in
sloppy ways. I think the challenge of making their own
interpretations helped students focus on the issues under discussion and enhanced their interest in the study
of Chinese history.

ADDENDUM: APRIL 1985

Soon after this column appeared, the Free Press
published the sourcebook mentioned in the article under
the title <u>Chinese Civilization and Society: A Source-
book</u>. In 1983 I wrote a <u>Teacher's Guide</u> for the sourcebook. The guide gives questions to ask students under
each selection, further readings, and practical suggestions for class discussion.

TO BEGIN WITH . . . EXERCISES IN HISTORIOGRAPHY

Julie Thompson Klein

January 1982

"The justification for history teaching does not lie in the acquisition of specified portions of the sum of fact. In mathematics or physics a pupil must master one skill before he can progress to another. Historical judgments are not built up in this way."

Martin Ballard

Historical literacy is a set of skills which is both sequential and expansive. Unlike the physics student, the history student does not master one set of calculations in order to progress towards more sophisticated algorithms. Still, if certain basic assumptions about history are not understood from the start, even the most rudimentary interpretations do not hold up. "History," as John Higham reminded us, "is common, but it is also complex." It would be foolish to argue that we can equip students with serviceable formulae for all their historical encounters. They must learn, as we do, to make adjustments for anomalies and unanticipated perspectives which defy even the soundest working principles. We can use, however, hands-on historiographical exercises which establish basic principles for thinking in time.

In my experiences with teaching historical and cross-cultural studies in both interdisciplinary and disciplinary settings, with both traditional and non-traditional students, I have devised a set of three exercises which have proven not only useful but also popular among students. Ideally, they should be used early and sequentially, though they could be separated and the original examples altered to correspond with individual syllabi. The historiographical exercises are defined as: problems of evidence; time and the language of historical records; the difference between describing and explaining.

I. Problems of Evidence

Rounding up objects or pictures of objects for students to examine is time well spent. As students attempt to draw conclusions from those objects, they are confronted with the possibilities and impossibilities of making interpretations based on evidence.

The British historian Peter Bamford used a particularly good scheme, assembling objects of a particular person in a particular time. A wallet is found, containing the following objects: a recent photograph of a young lady; a recent newspaper cutting of a wedding; a membership card of an exclusive golf club; two one-pound notes; a number of printed cards, with the same name and address on them; an Oxford class list (explain) of 1939; an airmail letter from Turkey; a DFC ribbon. Bamford then asked students who the owner of the wallet might have been.[1]

A similar exercise for other periods could be constructed by assembling photographs and drawings from a number of readily-available collections. I once assembled photographs and drawings to correspond with items that John Demos discusses in A Little Commonwealth: Family Life in Plymouth Colony. Students' discussion of those objects was animated and served as the base for considering problems of significance and verification. Students identified objects quickly but slowed down when asked to construct interpretations. As they proposed theories, I asked guiding questions which could be used with any objects. The questions were designed to involve students in the epistemology of historical interpretation.

What is the basis of your interpretation? Usually the answer involved a source: a book once read, a prior school lesson, a movie, a photograph or television program once seen, perhaps even a visit to a museum or historical site.

Is that source valid? The question is an excellent springboard for discussing problems of verification. Students can consider both traditional and non-traditional sources, the issues of objectivity and subjectivity in those sources and the limitations inherent in them.

How can one document an interpretation? This is a good way to open up discussion of verification to other students, who generally help out with other perspectives and further support.

II. The Time and Language of Historical Records

The value of an early exercise in writing history is worth repeating. Again, it is important to supply students with tangible material. During the second week of an American studies course, I presented students with the following:

> *Copies of the Old English poem "The Battle of Maldon" (which we read in a modern rendering, then discussed thematically);
>
> *The brief passage in the Anglo-Saxon Chronicle account of the 991 A.D. confrontation between English villagers at Maldon and victorious Viking invaders;
>
> *My research photographs of the battle site, with crucial sequencing of the alternately revealed and submerged causeway over which Vikings gained access to villagers and support troops;
>
> *A map of England;
>
> *Answers to their questions about the general history of Viking invasions as well as theories about the poem.

After presenting evidence and answering questions, I asked the class to write collectively a one-paragraph summary of the event for a history text. They felt quite confident about their ability to do so, resting upon what they considered an abundance of information. However, no later than the fourth word of the first sentence, students were arguing with each other about the wisdom or folly of particular words. After spending about ten minutes disputing such highly connotative and judgmental descriptions as "overwhelmed," "succumbed," and "brutalized," they decided to leave a few temporarily empty spaces in sentence one, then proceeded to sentence two. However, after another ten minutes of grappling with similar difficulties in their wording for sentence two, students realized the task of writing history was more complex than they had believed originally. Moreover, they had hands-on experience with the problem of language. For the remainder of the course, we were able to refer to our mutual exercise in writing history. In our collective experience there was a clear and strong lesson about word choice as an interpretative act. Neither were we to become Anglo-Saxon scholars nor was the Battle of Maldon relevant to the immediate course. However, the problems we had encountered were very relevant to our study of American history, in fact to any history.

Through the years, I increasingly have had students write out their interpretations. To help them resolve ambiguous problems or to moderate disputes, I offer to serve briefly as a scribe, writing on a chalkboard the sentences students construct. This is not only a good opportunity to discuss clear writing outside the English classroom, but also it enables students to benefit from each other's insights. Collective writing, then, works well not only in this specific exercise, but also at any point in a course where there is confusion and imprecision.

III. The Difference between Describing and Explaining

Whether used spontaneously or as part of a pre-planned, several-day exercise with student-assembled evidence, a simple question deserves asking. "What was the history of yesterday?" (For this idea, I thank Professor David Jacobs of Wayne State University, a humanities faculty member and coproducer of "An American Mosaic," an interdisciplinary telecourse in American studies.)

Yesterday is relatively accessible on any given day. It can be documented in a variety of ways: by memory, for a one-class discussion, or through tangible

resources for a longer period. However, as students
quickly discover, the question is simpler than the answer. As they offer answers, students experience a con-
flation of describer-explainer thinking. One group,
whose yesterday included a riot in Belfast, encountered
several problems which usually emerge in this exercise.
They realized that they had to distinguish immediately
between the who, what, where and when of reports and the
why's that were intermingled with simple descriptive
details. They then sorted out which details and comments belonged in the first or descriptive category and
which were interpretative explanations (again, with
their work visible on the chalkboard). Students found
that they had to shift items from one category to the
other when their differing qualities were realized. One
class decided to follow up on a yesterday event by seeking alternative explanations in various print sources.
We then made copies of those other reports and compared
the ratio of explanation to description and the posi-
tioning of description in relation to explanation.

As students sort out descriptions and explanations, they like using E. A. Peel's definition of the
four main aspects involved in the explainer's intellectual process: 1) the imagination of several possible
explanations; 2) the choice of one or more of them to
account for the problem being studied; 3) the systematic
elimination of unwanted alternatives; 4) deduction and
inference from hypotheses in relation to the data of the
problem.2

Using Peel's checklist helps students raise, defend, and dismiss interpretations in a more systematic
and productive manner and to appreciate with more depth
the lessons of exercise I, with its emphasis upon evidence, and exercise II, with its concern for language
choice.

The great reward for a teacher in using these exercises is the students' engagement in historiographical
problems, their active and energetic involvement in constructing theories, dismantling them where necessary,
and building up each other's interpretations. Student
eagerness to work in the third and fourth weeks of a
course is an outgrowth of earlier activity. The payoff

for everyone in the ninth and tenth weeks is the decline of basic errors. Exercise I tends to curb reductive judgments. Exercise II produces more critical word choices and class-wide attention to language. Reminding students of their experience with exercise III helps them see overgeneralizing, over-extended covering laws and overemphasis on similarities in not only their own thinking but also in sources they encounter. In short, they have learned to sort out better.

Partial evidence, linguistic limitations, and interpretative biases are certainly not the problems of historians alone, though they of course deal with specialized dimensions of those problems. By doing these exercises early in their study of history, students gain intellectual sensitivities which serve them well across the curriculum and beyond their school days. The majority of students in lower-level history courses will not become professional historians any more than most students in science classes will become professional scientists. The justification for literacy does not lie in that direction. It lies in the direction of teaching our students to recognize how their lives and the information they will gain are part of an historical process of enormous breadth and richness. In that they use historical thinking in their daily lives, they will realize how they need to exercise what we call historical judgments. In that they respect the complexity of historiographical problems, they will appreciate distinctions between their own historical literacy and the professional historian's craft.

[1]Peter Bamford, "Original Sources in the Classroom," New Movements in the Study and Teaching of History, 205.

[2]E. A. Peel, "Some Problems in the Psychology of History Teaching: II," Studies in the Nature and Teaching of History, 1983-84.

ADDENDUM: APRIL 1985

In the past few years we have witnessed the release of several well-publicized reports on the condition of modern secondary and higher education. Though

ranging over many subjects, each demonstrates a clear
concern for the quality of education today and a con-
comitant belief that we must concentrate on fundamental
"literacies." Alongside the predictable literacies
embodied in math and writing skills, some awareness of
history is always mentioned. We trust that the history
major will gain that literacy but have much less confidence about the majority of students, non-history majors. I have grown increasingly concerned about the
need for historical literacy in the general citizenry
because, like most of us, I continue to encounter skep-
ticism about studying the past alongside errors which
betray an ignorance of history. This sense of urgency
has only grown while teaching in a degree program for
adults who are for the most part returning to school
after an absence of time. As I see what has been forgotten or omitted in their prior learning, I understand
more than ever the importance of equipping them with
fundamental skills which are conveyed through engaging
and most of all participative activities in the classroom. Only by helping them teach themselves how to
respond to history and to make sound historical judgments can we insure that their new knowledge will not be
forgotten or sold back to the bookstore at semester's
end. Even with younger students I have taught, this
urgency is present, since the knowledge and critical
skills which they decide to retain now will have a life-
long effect on their values and actions. Rooting the
information of a course in a basic set of critical activities increases the chances of both remembering and
valuing the lessons of that course, not just "what"
those lessons are but "how" and "why" we are doing them.

I no longer use the Maldon example per se but try
to adapt the basic technique of writing history described in section II ("The Time and Language of Historical Records") to an example from the current text in
a given course. While teaching "Historical Perspectives," an upper-level course which focuses on the epistemology of historical knowledge, I adapt these exercises to a rich variety of case studies in the James
West Davidson and Mark Hamilton Lytle collection After
the Fact, The Art of Historical Detection (New York:
Alfred Knopf, 1982), in addition to an extended class
case study on the frontier in American society. The

controlling questions of Section I ("Problems of Evidence") and the four main aspects of the explainer's intellectual process in Section III ("The Difference between Describing and Explaining") are so fundamental to clear critical thinking that I now use them to one degree or another in any course I teach. I was delightfully surprised recently to learn that one of the professional historians I originally consulted about historical pedagogy now uses the set of exercises I devised in his own history courses, finding them to be excellent ways of helping his students to develop a sound set of historiographical skills. For both the major and the non-major, then, integrating these basic exercises with course content increases the chances of rooting the study of history in a set of fundamental intellectual skills.

DOING ORAL HISTORY: THE YOUNTVILLE PROJECT

Jacqueline B. Barnhart

December 1980

Recently, I directed a group of students at California State University, Chico in a biographical oral history project at the Veterans' Home of California at Yountville. I am convinced that it was a profitable experience both for the students and their instructor. In fact, the project was beneficial not only in acquiring the skills of doing oral biography but also in developing a greater understanding of the nature of history.

The Yountville home is one of the largest of its kind in the country and thus offered a potentially rich opportunity for an oral history project. The institution houses 1400 residents in a variety of accommodations. There is a 400-bed hospital that has the potential of becoming one of the best geriatric facilities in the nation. There are annexes for those veterans who require nursing care or special medical aid. However, most residents live in private rooms or dormitory wards in the resident halls of Yountville. To be eligible for Yountville, one must have served in the United States military in a time of conflict and have some kind of service-related disability, a vague term which includes everything from injury to such disorders as heart trouble or nervous conditions. The average age of the veterans is seventy-five, and they represent every war from the Spanish-American to Vietnam.

Being a novice in the field but a reasonably careful scholar, I did a good deal of research in the methods of oral history. I wanted to be thoroughly prepared before beginning the project. I read the handouts on oral history and found Willa Baum's, Oral History for the Local Historical Society, most useful.[1] In addition, I attended an oral history session at a regional historians' conference and sought the advice of a number of scholars experienced in the field.

Out of this expertise, one message was heard again

and again: the interviewer must be prepared for problems that are certain to develop. Forethought and proper planning can minimize difficulties but not eliminate them altogether--as we were soon to find out. In spite of concerted efforts to keep equipment in good working order, tapes did break, recorder batteries went dead, and outside noises interfered with taping sessions. And occasionally the interviewer forgot to flip the tape to a new side in the middle of the most interesting segment of an interview. We found a sense of humor and good rapport with the veterans indispensable in dealing with difficulties of this sort.

Another problem we encountered was the suddenly recalcitrant subject. Explanations for this kind of behavior varied from fatigue and ineffective techniques to poor chemistry between subject and interviewer. Although no sure solution emerged, we did determine several ways of avoiding or adapting to the situation.

We found that when talking with elderly individuals the interviewer had to watch for fatigue and prepare, if necessary, to postpone the interview to a later time. One hour was about the maximum amount of time a session could be sustained comfortably. Keep in mind that this is not a casual conversation and demands great concentration. The subject is aware of the tape recorder and concerned with having something of interest and importance to say.

We also discovered that a weary interviewer could doom a profitable taping session. While planning the project, it was my intention to spend four or five days conducting intensive taping sessions. After the first day this plan was dropped. It was impossible to conduct more than two or three interviews in a day. The energy expended during an interview is comparable to reading a highly technical article. The tape does not do the listening. It is necessary to be alert and ready to follow up on half-made references and tentative responses. In short, one has to listen.

Yet to listen is more difficult than it seems. A part of the mind is always on the tape and mechanical problems that might occur. In the first few hours of interviews, it is almost impossible to be comfortable with blank space--taped "dead air"--while the subject is thinking. And the tendency is to think ahead and formulate the next question while the present one is being answered. Finally, some subjects are just plain boring; it is hard to maintain even minimal interest until the interview can be terminated gracefully. If the lack of concentration and interest is obvious, the session will likely deteriorate into monosyllabic responses.

Although an hour was about the average length for an interview, we had to keep our schedules flexible. For example, one student went back three times to see a subject and taped about twenty minutes of conversation each time. The veteran, a double amputee and bedridden, could tolerate only a twenty minute visit without rest. On the other hand, I interviewed a man born in 1896. At the end of the fourth hour of tape, he had reached only 1948 in his biographical narrative and, short of walking away, there was no way for me to limit the interview.

Experience revealed that the most productive interview was the one with the least number of questions and interruptions. Too frequent promptings or introduction of new topics interrupted the memory process and thus produced little material. Moreover, aside from confusing the subjects, one risked antagonizing them. Seventy and eighty year olds are often apologetic about being slow to remember. To interrupt them repeatedly reinforces their fear that they are slow and dull-witted. If that happens, resentment will end all prospects for a good interview. Patience, then, should be added to listening as a vital ingredient in the oral historian's bag.

Difficulties between the interviewer and subject occasionally were responsible for the breakdown of a taping session. If the "chemistry" was bad, the interviewer either shut off the tape recorder and tried to overcome whatever bad feelings had developed or requested that another person continue the interview at the next session. We tried each of these approaches at one time or another, and one of them usually worked. But whichever approach was used, a full and honest discussion of the difficulties was helpful: the subject felt

less inadequate and often was instrumental in solving
the problems.

This was roughly the procedure I used to save a
potentially excellent interview from complete disaster.
Though most of those we talked to at Yountville were
past seventy years old, I did interview one thirty year
old Vietnam veteran. He was a willing subject and, since
he was of my generation, conversation should have been
easy. However, quickly the interview deteriorated into
a yes, a no, or a shrug in response to my questions.
Finally, I shut off the tape recorder, admitted I was at
a loss to know what had happened, and felt I had somehow
antagonized him. He denied this without conviction; it
occurred to me that this was indeed a matter of chemistry. As far as I know, I had revealed nothing about my
attitude concerning the Vietnam War but he sensed that I
had opposed the war. On the other hand, he did not make
moral judgments about the war. His attitude, which he
later explained, was "If your country was involved then
you fought." I spent ten minutes explaining my views
and making it clear that I had no intention of being
judgmental. I just wanted to understand his experiences
and feelings. When I finished my explanation and turned
the recorder on again, I obtained the most perceptive
interview that I had received thus far. In other situa-
tions this approach might have failed; as a general
rule, I do not think the interviewer should give opinions or relate personal experiences. Subjects will
often not bother to elaborate on a topic when they think
the interviewer is already in agreement. When they hold
different views, they might avoid disagreement for the
sake of peace or good manners. However, in the Vietnam
veteran's case, there was nothing to lose and the results were fruitful.

An additional problem encountered in doing biographical histories has to do with age. There are, of
course, the technical problems of taping someone ninety
years old whose voice is unintelligible on tape or who
has intermittent days of mental clarity and physical
energy. One student was scheduled to interview a man
who was reported to have a fascinating history. When
the student arrived for the taping session, he was taken
into the subject's bathroom, ordered not to turn on the

recorder, and told an incoherent tale of conspiracy and spying. Problems of this type must be expected.

Most of the veterans we taped were between seventy and eighty-five years of age. It soon was clear that we had to do little more than start the tape by saying, "Tell me about your life--where and when were you born?" We only interrupted when it was necessary to obtain additional details. What was not expected was that the request for a biography of anyone under seventy was considered almost an insult, and the response was often "There isn't much to tell." In these cases, it was necessary to ask specific questions. The interviews were lucid, but they lacked the spontaneity of the narrative biography.

There are a number of explanations for this phenomenon. Foremost is the fact that most people do not think of themselves as old while in their sixties, and they resent being asked for their life story since this suggests that their life is over. However, to live to the age of seventy and beyond is seen as an admirable accomplishment. Those who live to this revered age are encouraged, even expected, to pass along the wisdom which they have acquired over the years. To be sure, this was the situation at Yountville where the primary criterion for "venerable" status is age.

The problems we encountered might occur in any oral history project. It is possible that they are more prevalent in the type of project conducted at Yountville where we took a biographical rather than a topical approach. The latter lends itself to greater organization about specific thematic questions. But this kind of approach was not workable at Yountville. The fact that everyone there had been in the military in time of conflict did not even provide a unifying theme. Few of the residents were "career military." Most of them served their hitches and got out. Often the least significant years of their lives were those spent in the services. As a result, we have an hour of interesting information of the experiences of a song-and-dance man on the Orpheum Circuit; two hours on the activities of a Bonus Army participant; details of the "Polar Bear" campaign of World War I; the memories of a POW in Germany during the last months of World War II; combat experiences in Cuba in 1898; the Vera Cruz invasion of 1913; Argonne in World War I; Iwo Jima in World War II; descriptions of the work of a journalist-photographer, nurse, female private investigator, military cook, engineer, pilot, cavalry soldier, gunner, and aerial photographer. These and the other stories we collected are interesting. Yet none is a complete story on any subject. When the tapes are transcribed and available for distribution, they will be a valuable adjunct to various topics of research. To me, this is the best use of oral history.*

Learning to cope with the problems mentioned above was a valuable experience for all of us. An additional by-product was that the project provided a graphic illustration that history is interpretive. For example, the students confidently asked questions about the Great Depression, expecting to hear stories of "Hoovervilles," hobos, and soup lines; as often as not, they learned that, if a man had a job during the period, he was only vaguely aware of the depression. The students discovered that a minor battle in the history books was often a life-changing event for the individual firing the machine gun. In short, they learned the kind of lesson every history instructor tries to impart: not only is history interpretive but historical memory also varies according to one's perspective.

As a final note, I urge anyone teaching an oral history class or planning an oral history project to consider carefully the value of local biographical history that is available at veterans' homes or similar institutions. There is a rich vein of precious material just waiting to be tapped by any student of social history. Don't let it go to waste.

----

[1]Willa Baum, Oral History for the Local Historical Society (Nashville, Tenn.: American Association for State and Local History, 1974, 2nd revised edition).

*In the spring of 1981 an annotated list of interviews and transcripts was available at a small charge through Special Collections, LARC, California State University-Chico, Chico, CA 95929.

NEW PERSPECTIVES ON USING THE LIBRARY
IN HISTORY TEACHING

E. A. Reitan

April 1978

In the 1976-77 academic year I held a half-time position with the new Teaching-Learning Center, partially funded by a grant from the Kellogg Foundation, at Illinois State University. Part of my assignment was to develop a series of workshops bringing together departmental faculty and library staff in a series of workshops dealing with the instructional uses of the library. I found the assignment a congenial one. Historians are library people. The historian is most truly himself when he enters the library in search of answers to historical questions, and like every other historian, I have spent many happy hours in a wide variety of libraries.

As the workshops unfolded, a natural sequence of thought emerged. The first stage I call the operational stage, which was mainly concerned with how the system worked. Faculty wanted to talk about acquisitions in their fields of special interest, or to discuss such custodial questions as putting books on reserve or preventing students from cutting articles out of journals. Faculty, I found, were not using this stage primarily as an opportunity to vent grievances. They were genuinely interested in the library, and they were showing their concern by bringing up questions which grew out of their interest in the smooth functioning of the system. And the librarians, if given half a chance, would talk all day about such problems. In this respect, I was enormously impressed with the competence of our library staff. They were way ahead of faculty in identifying and dealing with these problems. It was good for faculty to find that problems which were frustrating or irritating were not only understood but being dealt with.

The second natural stage for the workshops I called the instructional process stage. Essentially

what was involved here was consideration of the ways in
which teachers and librarians worked with students to
help them carry out library assignments. When librarians
responded to this subject they thought in the conventional terms of library instruction: "nuts and bolts"
matters of using the card catalog, identifying and using
the necessary reference tools, finding the books, etc.
The librarians obviously see this need as an important
part of their duties, but my concern was to get faculty
thinking about their role in the process. It seemed
clear to me that the major role of classroom teachers
was to deal with those aspects of library use which were
distinctive to their subjects. Since the usual library
orientation given to freshmen is of a general nature,
the history teacher should assume responsibility for
bringing his students into contact with the special resources and special techniques needed to use the library
for historical studies. It is here that the technical
expertise of the librarian cannot replace the professional know-how and informed instinct of the trained
historian.

Two major problems emerged in this stage of the
workshops: 1) many faculty were quite offhand in giving
library assignments, and 2) most faculty did not concern
themselves much with how the student carried out the
assignment once it was given. Consequently, librarians
were required to assume such responsibilities of the
teacher as helping the students define the topic, identifying the relevant reference tools in an area where
the teacher (presumably) possessed expertise, or even
trying to determine from the garbled account given by
the student what the assignment actually was. For the
first time I discovered how student use of the library
appeared from the library perspective, and I heard
enough horror stories to last a lifetime. It may be
some consolation to a group of historians to learn that
the worst examples came from business, education, industrial arts, and physical education, but I could not
avoid squirming as I imagined how some of my own students must have floundered when a little more direction
on my part would have made the difference. It seemed
evident that if faculty would give clear and well-
defined assignments in written form, and give the students reasonable help in defining the topic and locating

materials, many library problems would be eliminated or substantially reduced. In short, in this respect, as in so many other aspects of the instructional process, we must ask faculty to take time to be teachers.

The third stage of the workshops was my principal interest, but it was difficult to get faculty or librarians to the point of thinking clearly about it. This was the stage of thinking about the library as it related to instructional_goals. The paramount goal of most faculty, as demonstrated by what they do, regardless of what they may say, is to communicate to students what is known--or at least what they know--about the subject they teach. There is nothing wrong with this goal per se, and obviously the library has an important role to play in accomplishing it. But teachers should go beyond mere communication of information. They should lead students to think about the problems which arise in their subject, and help students develop the attitudes and skills needed to find information and resolve these problems. My goal was to encourage faculty to foster in their students a spirit of inquiry which would lead them to the library as the greatest repository of information and ideas. I cannot say that our workshops got very far in achieving this goal, but perhaps they accomplished something.

But there was another aspect of this third stage which was made abundantly clear by the experience of the librarians and the faculty. They discovered that many students are frightened by the library and often prefer to use departmental libraries, hometown public libraries, or their own personal books. Few faculty have really worked to resolve this fear; many have given in to it as the course of least resistance. Some of this fear of libraries is rooted in technological developments of our age which have diminished the role of books in the lives of many families. To some extent this fear grows out of the giantism of our universities, the impersonality of instruction, and the complexity of modern knowledge, to which the library is no exception. Students are afraid of the unknown, and the library is more unknown and unknowable than ever before. Expert assistance from librarians will help, but to the students, the librarians are strangers. It is primarily the role of the teacher to lead the students, in a firm, helpful, and kindly manner to explore the unknown library and feel comfortable in it. Instruction in the "nuts and bolts" of library usage is important. It is necessary that library assignments be interesting, clearly explained, and within the capacity of the students. But most important is an approach to instruction which emphasizes the pursuit of knowledge rather than the absorption of it--the spirit of inquiry rather than dependence upon the authority of the teacher or the textbook. Perhaps our workshops helped some faculty to become more aware of the challenge they face in bringing students to a love of learning and helping them to find in the library the resources essential to their quest.

How can the experience of these workshops be applied to the teaching of history? I begin with the assumption that the goal of history teaching is to enable students to develop historical imagination and that the best way to accomplish that goal is to call upon them to do what historians do. No one who observes the teaching of history in American universities, colleges, or community colleges can doubt that the reality of history teaching is far from Carl Becker's ideal of "every man his own historian." If history teachers and students continue to emphasize historical information at the expense of historical thinking, the essential purpose of history teaching will be lost. Historical knowledge is needed as a foundation for historical inquiry, but unless the doing of history and the learning of history are combined, it is likely that neither will be done very well. Obviously the library has a role to play in the mastery of history's content, but textbooks and anthologies can go far in satisfying that need. It is in the inquiry aspect of historical instruction that the library is the essential resource and the use of the library the essential skill.

The principal error of history teachers is the unfounded assumption that because they know how to use the library in their research, they also know how to use the library in teaching. Of course, the professional historian knows a lot about libraries. He has spent much of his life in them. But this experience in libraries has given him little grasp of how students perceive and use libraries. The history teacher needs to ask what steps he or she would follow if called upon to write on an historical subject outside his or her field of expertise. The steps include: general reading to grasp the historical context of the subject; gradually formulating, defining, and limiting the topic; learning the bibliographical tools and building a bibliography; discovering the primary sources available; noting the prominent historians in the field; and studying the major problems of interpretation. The next time you give a library assignment, go to the library and replicate the steps that you think the students should follow. Then ask them to list the steps they actually followed. And take it from there.

An approach to history teaching which makes full use of the library will require close cooperation between the faculty and the librarians. Most librarians are eager for such cooperation. The most elemental step is to inform the librarian before the term begins of the demands which will be made upon the library for each course. Bibliographies, reading lists, and library assignments should be sent to the librarian to be available when answering student questions. A more useful procedure would be to plan the course, especially as it relates to the library, with the librarian, who can contribute his special expertise to the process and who will be more able to help the students. If such procedures are followed, a visit by the librarian to the class when the assignments are made could be useful, for then the students would know that there was a friendly face in the library. Custodial policies should also be discussed with the librarian, including special reserve needs, access to periodicals or unusual collections, and attractive displays in the lobby. Such an approach to teaching will also affect the faculty member's attitude toward acquisitions. Of course, it will continue to be important for the library to order books, periodicals, and source materials for the faculty member's research and graduate seminar, as well as for his personal growth. But a survey of instructional needs will reveal quite different acquisition problems, including multiple copies and source materials which are easily usable. Faculty leadership in library use has been lost primarily by default. Faculty involvement in library poli-

cies, assistance to students, and acquisitions will return this essential, and extremely costly, instructional
resource to serving the instructional purpose of the
faculty.

As I observed the series of library workshops offered at Illinois State University by our new Teaching-
Learning Center, I felt I learned something very important. As we consider the new instructional resources
available in our age of technological wonders, the most
important resource is misused or underutilized, simply
because it is so obvious. It is time to take another
look at the instructional uses of the library.

V. THE NEW HISTORY

TEACHING WOMEN'S HISTORY

Gerda Lerner

May/June 1976

The number of colleges and universities offering separate programs in women's studies is steadily rising; in 1975 there were 152 such programs reported. According to a recent article in The Chronicle of Higher Education, 39 institutions offer a B.A. in women's studies, 11 offer an M.A., and 3 offer a Ph.D. Women's history is an integral part of all these women's studies programs. Additionally, many institutions without such programs are regularly offering women's history courses; the last reported number of women's history courses was 4658. (See editor's note updating these figures on page 99.)

Women's history can be taught at different levels and from a variety of perspectives. Those teaching women's history have over the past five years acquired some experience and developed techniques which might be useful to others. All or some of the approaches discussed below are currently being used by teachers.

Compensatory and contribution history. Where are the women? What did they contribute to American history? These are the questions asked in an effort to find the "missing" women, their achievements, their organizations, and to incorporate them into traditional course outlines.

This approach is useful for an introduction to the subject. College students usually have difficulty naming ten important women active before 1950 (or ten events important to women) whereas they can easily name ten men in history. This fact demonstrates how little learning pertaining to women students have acquired in their early years of education, and also makes students aware of their dependence on historians' interpretations of history. It easily leads to discussions of historiography and of value judgments in historical scholarship. Once students become interested in finding out more about the largest group of "anonymous" in history, they can be

involved in the search for the "missing women" and their
activities.   Some teachers have used the technique of
assigning one or two women for study to each student.
As the students become expert on their subjects, they
are asked to bring the material they have studied into
relationship with the class readings in traditional
textbooks, in which women barely appear at all.

Compensatory history has the disadvantage that
women inevitably appear in the "also ran" category,
their activities and importance contrasted and ranked
below the recognized and accredited achievements of men
in politics, warfare and state-craft.   This pitfall can
be avoided by teachers' awareness that such judgments
represent the existence of unspoken patriarchal assumptions.   These can at least be discussed and opened up to
evaluation by asking questions such as: "The men were
fighting the war; what was it like for women?"   "We know
what frontier life was like for men; what was it like
for women?"

Women's history separated from general history.
This teaching approach is probably the one most commonly
used today in women's studies programs.   Special courses
are offered on a variety of subjects all of which focus
on women, separate women from the general population
and, frequently, deal with the oppression of women and
their response to it as a device for organizing the
material.   In some cases, students study women from the
vantage point of several disciplines, either in interdisciplinary lecture courses or in separate seminars
which deal with women in history, the image of women in
literature, the psychology of women, etc. The advantage
of this approach is that it allows students to acquire
an overview of the field and to compensate, usually in a
one-semester course, for the past neglect of women in
history.   The disadvantage is inherent in just that
assumption.   Women's history can no more be "acquired"
in a one-semester course or a year's course than can
American history or French history.   While many women,
feminist and non-feminist, feel that it is necessary and
desirable to teach women's history in separate programs,
for a time, only the fewest would maintain that such a
separation should be long sustained.   It is a necessary
first step in undoing past neglect and in calling atten-

tion to the complexities of the problem, but it should not remain the only step taken by departments of history and by the profession as a whole.

Women as a minority or marginal group. Another approach taken to the teaching of women's history is to treat women as a subgroup and to lump them together with other minorities, sometimes even in courses specifically called "Minorities in U.S. History." The intent is to somehow incorporate women in the structure of history programs as currently taught and organized. It is probably better to deal with the subject this way than it is to ignore it altogether. Still, the effect of such an approach is to reinforce and perpetuate the patronizing assumption that women, as a group, are marginal to historical development. But women are and always have been half of the population and their activities have always been an essential and integral part of the history of the country. Women have experienced educational, legal and economic discrimination as have members of minority groups, but they, unlike truly marginal groups, are distributed through every group and class of society and have also functioned with males of their group and class. Therefore, they must be treated and discussed as fullfledged partners in history and their historic role must be interpreted and understood as such.

Gender added as an analytical category to social history. When gender is considered with race, class, ethnicity and religious affiliation an entirely new dimension is added to social history. How were women affected by changes in family life, employment patterns, education, law and institutional structures? How were women subordinated and how did they respond to such subordination? How were social values affected by this process? These and similar questions yield much information about women and families and throw a new light on traditional interpretations.

Changes in sexual mores, prescriptive behavior and sex-role indoctrination are similarly taken into consideration when analyzing and discussing different historical periods.

Many women's history courses are structured around

topics concerned with the image of women at a given
time. Literary sources, popular periodicals and travelers' accounts are used to give a lively picture of the
way women appeared to contemporaries. This is fine as
far as it goes, but historical understanding deepens
when the image of women in a given period is contrasted
with the actual status of women. This kind of assignment usually shows up an important gap between image and
reality. Gaining awareness of this fact is of particular significance for the history of women since women
are so much subject to social control and social indoctrination.

Thus the literature of domesticity occurs at a
time when women in large numbers are leaving the home to
work in the early factories. The romantic fiction ex-
tolling the Southern lady appears in a period when the
old plantation system has been destroyed and industri-
alization is advancing upon the South. In the twentieth
century, the role of advertising and of the media in
influencing the decisions women make and the attitudes
of society toward women is more complex and certainly
worth studying. Studies of sexual stereotypes in the
mass media and in popular culture can be usefully combined with readings on the legal and social status of
women and on shifts in their occupations and economic
function. Such assignments prove to be challenging to
students; they are appropriate for students in seminars
as well as survey courses.

Reconstructing the female experience. Based on
the consideration that the female point of view deserves
to be treated equally with that of males in reconstructing the past, this approach leads to a search for new
sources and eventually for new principles of organizing
historical materials. Teachers and their students begin
to examine the hidden assumption, which now pervades all
historical writing as it does our culture, that man is
the measure of all values and that women are outsiders
to historical events, affected by them, but not deci-
sively affecting them. Inevitably, such a teaching approach leads to comparisons between the historical experience of men and that of women and to a new synthesis.
What did the past mean to men, what to women? How did
their experience of particular events--such as revolu-

tion, wars, depressions--differ? Or did it differ at all? What were the activities of men and women at given times in the past, and how did they affect historical events? What were significant periods of change for men, for women These are some of the questions which will elicit information about women and their participation in history.

Regardless of the approach historians take, this new angle of vision offers certain advantages to the teaching of history. Women's history leads the student to the use of primary sources; it makes historiography come alive; it encourages student involvement with historical studies.

Use of primary sources. The long neglect of women in history is most evident in the absence of sound monographic studies on women. The many dissertations now being done will, in a short time, fill this gap. Meanwhile, teachers are forced--perhaps fortuitously--to use primary sources. These are abundantly available to the teacher in the form of autobiographies, diaries and letters--sources also used for family history. Many of these materials are available in reprints or on microfilm. By making use of reference works like the indispensable Notable American Women, students can be taught the rudiments of preparing a bibliography and of doing biographical research. Students can learn to verify information in assignments built around some notable women, which then can form the basis for the study of selected groups--abolitionists, builders of institutions, teachers, progressive reformers in which the career and life patterns, achievements, and style of work of a group of women are compared with those of a similar group of men.

Historiography comes alive. As teachers ask questions pertinent to women, students become involved in the critique and evaluation of sources. Teachers can stimulate students to seek an understanding of historiography by discussing shifting emphases, viewpoints and historical interpretations in the history of women. This greatly enhances student interest in history as a field of study, as can be seen by the generally high enrollment figures in women's history courses.

Student involvement with the subject. Women's
history, like family history, makes it possible to link
personal history--that of the students' families--with
that of reference groups such as immigrants, workers and
members of a religious group. Students can be taught
the essentials of verification by having them check information obtained through oral history techniques--
interviews with parents or relatives--against data from
printed sources such as birth and marriage records, nat-
uralization documents, etc. Background readings on im-
migration or ethnic groups connect such assignments with
traditional textbook units.

Similar assignments, in which students can study
the life patterns and work participation of women in
their family, can be combined with the reading of articles on demographic history, family history, history of
childrearing and labor history, and these can be followed by readings which provide the historical background. This educational approach, which allows students to learn historical method by participating in the
work of the historian-scholar in an introductory way,
arouses the interest of students and demonstrates to
them the connection between their lives, their society,
their past. It elevates the study of history from a
"dry subject" (as students often regard it) to a subject
essential for understanding and self-development.

Every community, local history society, and library is a storehouse of information about the activities of women. The records of women's organizations, of
churches, schools, and hospitals contain much information about the lives, activities, and concerns of women
of the past. Local newspapers yield information about
women, not only in their columns and "women's pages",
but in advertisements, letters to the editor and business news. Students at any level of proficiency can
work with such primary sources. Assignments, such as
trying to discover whether there were any business and
professional women in a given locality fifty or more
years ago or studying the career patterns of a group of
female graduates of an academy or women's college, are
helpful and often lead students to take considerable
initiative in finding answers to open-ended questions.

Finally, a word should be said about the importance of women's history to female students. For them, women's history means studying a subject which directly involves their sense of identity and their adjustment to society, work and family. The long neglect of women in history reflects cultural neglect, which has had a serious effect on the intellectual functioning of women in a predominantly male university setting. Educators have been as insensitive to the subtle effects on academic achievement of discrimination against women as they were in earlier years to the effects on academic achievement of discrimination against blacks. Assuming that equality of opportunity was sufficient, they have tended to disregard the long heritage of injury to self-esteem, of lack of self-assurance, and of confusion about conflicting demands made by society upon the young woman and by the young woman upon herself. By the time they reach college, most girls have been conditioned to subordinate their curiosity, initiative, and particularly their female reactions and insights to the standards imposed upon them by the dominant culture. Added to this must be the serious long-range effect upon any group of persons who are denied knowledge of and access to a legitimate past. Learning to uncover the past of women becomes for most female students an exhilarating intellectual experience and often helps to raise their self-esteem and increase their educational motivation.

The large numbers of women in colleges and universities is a guarantee that interest in women's history will continue to grow. Society's changing cultural values in regard to women and sex roles in general, make the full incorporation of women's history into historical studies an educational necessity. Women's history-- far from fading away--is a new and growing field, one which can do much toward invigorating and revitalizing the teaching of history.

(Editor's note: The National Women's Studies Association lists about 600 colleges and universities now offering programs in women's studies. Approximately 250 of these award a B.A. or B.S., 55 an M.A., and 19 a Ph.D. Five of the institutions award Ph.D.'s through departments of history.)

PROBLEMS OF DEFINITION IN ENVIRONMENTAL HISTORY

Thad W. Tate

May/June 1981

In an effort to establish environmental history as a distinct field of historical study, environmental historians are participating in a process of fragmentation that has increasingly characterized the study and teaching of history. For better or for worse, the older, more conventional categorizations of history by nation or region and by long recognized aspects of political, social, economic, or intellectual conduct is now reinforced--some might say splintered--by a confusing variety of new or newly emphasized approaches. One hopes, of course, that this fragmentation of history is not, as some might suggest, a mark of increasing disintegration. Rather those of us involved in this process proceed in the hope that our activity gives evidence of a breadth and openness that will in the end reinvigorate the study of history. There are signs, too, that the tendency toward fragmentation need not be permanent but may instead, as the work of the Annales school in French and European history suggests, eventuate in a new and richer synthesis of historical understanding.

Nonetheless, fragmentation is for the present an overriding fact, with or without the addition of environmental history. For the most part these newer fields of study--women's history, black history, American Indian history, historical demography, psycho history, to cite but a few examples--elicit more or less instant recognition of their approach and content. To say, however, that one teaches, or proposes to teach, environmental history, is to invite the opposite reaction, to draw a quizzical look at best, if not an explicit request for explanation. Very few of these new approaches to history--the burgeoning field of public history comes most readily to mind as another possibility--seem to raise similar doubts. Some of the implicit scepticism can be attributed to the innate traditionalism of historians, distrust of the "trendy," and suspicion that many environmental historians operate in an excessive spirit of advocacy. More important, there is little doubt that the subject of environmental history raises sufficiently legitimate problems of definition, organization, and methodology to make the scepticism understandable.

One of these problems rises from the difficulty of achieving balance and perspective in the face of the unusual fervor and commitment that draws scholars to environmental history. The environmental movement has increasingly taken on many of the characteristics of a crusade, and it is probably not unfair to suggest that most environmental historians share the moral and ethical concerns of that movement. The combination of our own beliefs and those of many of the students who elect to attend our courses may sometimes do more to strengthen this deep commitment than to develop a detached historical perspective. The long-term credibility of environmental history, however, is dependent on the attainment of proper scholarly detachment.

Environmentalists themselves are not, and have never been, of one accord; they come in varied guises from conservationists who retain a faith in technological solutions to the most radical and utopian Turtle Islanders who despair altogether of political solutions. Those of us who profess to be environmental historians owe it to the subject, therefore, to analyze and explain, as best we can the entire range of human actions and responses on matters affecting the environment and to do so in a way that does not simply divide the world into villains and heroes. Environmental history is more than the history of a crusade, even if it is in part that too. To call for such detachment is not to strip the subject of all passion and conviction. After all, much of the limited but growing body of explicitly anti-environmental literature is, if anything, more outspoken and more polemical than even the most frenzied pro-environmental writing. A proper historical perspective must recognize the existing depth of feeling and the consequent tendency to define the debate in moral and ethical as much as technical and scientific terms. But it may also assess the meaning of that phenomenon objectively, not become a party to it. We must remember that the current debate is but one part of a complex and varied set of human interactions with nature.

The character of the contemporary environmental debate poses a second problem as well in that the views of many modern environmentalists seem to reflect a radical break with the past rather than the culmination of some logical pattern of historical development. If we accept the terms of the debate at all literally, many environmentalists are telling us that modern technology is capable not merely of inflicting environmental damage and resource depletion but of causing the destruction of the human race itself and that the threat demands a radically transformed culture, not simply political reforms or improved technology. Not everyone, of course, agrees with an argument of such extremity, but the issue has been joined with an unprecedented sense of urgency.

When one contrasts, moreover, the staggering quantity of post-1950 literature on environmental issues-- both the technical and professional writing and the popular statements of a Barry Commoner or a Rachel Carson-- with the paucity of earlier work, particularly that which antedates the much milder conservationist arguments of the early twentieth century, there is additional reason to suspect that the environmental question as we now understand it might have a limited historical dimension. But to the contrary I think I am prepared to maintain that this heightened attention to environmental relationships, as yet certainly incomplete but almost as certainly irreversible, offers clear evidence of a profound shift in understanding and attitude that cuts deeply into the existing culture. The particular form of gnawing apprehension that we label environmental may well intersect with other aspects of an even more pervasive social and cultural malaise. Yet there are a range of problems--energy and resources, population, pollution, the effects of toxic substances, the imminent disappearance of the last vestiges of an undisturbed natural world--that have come to be widely understood as having fundamental implications for almost every aspect of life. Although doubters, of course, remain, environmental debate now occurs less frequently between those who see a threat and those who dismiss it entirely than between those who see the crisis with differing degrees of urgency and those who embrace or reject more advanced technology as a solution.

If the whole question is indeed as vital and urgent as it genuinely appears to be, the argument that
the environmental issue justifies searching historical
investigation in its own right becomes all the more
pressing. If the break with the past is as sharp as it
at first seemed, one has to assume that such a circum-
stance is in itself a phenomenon that deserves to be
understood in historical terms, and although revolutions
in history generally prove to be more evolutionary and
more linked to the past than at first appears, in this
instance the confusion may arise from our preoccupation
with the moral and ethical dimensions of the current
controversy. The means by which one can establish the
continuities, and at the same time appraise more accurately the degree of novelty in the present situation,
lies first, of course, in giving full weight to a wider
range of responses and in shifting our emphasis somewhat
off the single matter of perceived crises so that we can
look much more broadly at the ongoing relationship between humans and nature. Historians are always drawn to
crises, yet the larger truth in this case is that there
is, after all, in all periods of history a range of
human relationship to nature, involving many kinds of
actions, perceptions, and unspoken assumptions. As
historians, then, we should avoid becoming enmeshed in
what seems novel or particularly urgent in the present
and undertake instead a broader investigation of the
full range of past human responses to the natural environment. While the risks of advocacy and present-
mindedness are certainly present, they do not so much
destroy the justification for treating environmental
history as a distinct thematic field as they impose on
it an unusually strong demand for reasonable detachment
and objectivity and for a sense of historical perspective that is best gained by viewing the process of human
interaction with nature as broadly as possible.

To call for this degree of breadth in the study
and teaching of environmental history is to raise--and
perhaps compound--an even more fundamental problem, that
of how to define the field within manageable limits. We
have--properly in my judgment--now made the relationship
between people and environment into one of the most all-
encompassing of all human concerns. The totality of the
relationship is at once the most compelling justifica-

tion for the study of environmental history and the root of the problem of defining that study. One runs the risk of having to regard all human history as in some degree environmental in nature, even if one escapes the hazard of imparting a crude environmental determinism to human affairs.

In the end I suspect most college-level courses in environmental history have been formulated on a hit-or-miss basis; I concede my own has. We put them together to reflect our personal interests and to draw on some favorite reading. Our emphasis is likely to be on the intellectual dimension of the subject. From the beginning of recorded history humans have possessed some network of sensory perceptions, attitudes, and, ultimately, consciously formulated ideas about the natural world; religious and aesthetic views of nature, both wild and cultivated; moral and ethical definitions of their relationships with the natural world; or some understanding of how they should act toward the land on which they live. Indeed the particular form these assumptions and ideas have assumed in a given culture and their change over time remain one of the best gauges of the way in which a whole range of environmental relationships are understood at given times in history. My plea is simply that we not rely too heavily on this aspect of the subject.

A second dimension, equally obvious but one that perhaps deserves greater emphasis and more detailed consideration than it often receives, can most conveniently be defined as technological. I use the term here in an extremely broad way that comprehends a good deal more than simply the impact of more recent and advanced forms of industrial activity. Rather I employ it in the sense that humans may be said to have possessed a technology of sorts from the time a man first shaped a stone tool or made a conscious effort to assemble a food supply. The point is to lay down as an operating principle that all human actions affecting nature are modifications of the environment, some beneficial or at least innocuous and some harmful. Because we are in a hurry to get on to the results of, and reactions to, environmental manipulation, because the sources are difficult to use, and because we lack an accessible literature, we find it difficult to provide systematic consideration of the physical and material aspects of human modifications of the natural world.

I would single out a third dimension, science as distinct from the applied science of technology, as another ingredient of our definition. There has always been some curiosity about the natural world but this inquiry took on somewhat greater significance and precision with the advent of Darwinian science and with the subsequent development of ecology. Only then was the scientific dimension sufficiently developed to make possible a more precise understanding and measurement of the physical environment. Although technology must supply some of the techniques, ecology provides the standards for measuring the network of human interaction with the environment and for understanding the possibilities for extreme modification and destruction that are inherent in the relationship.

But historians, even as they recognize that the adaptation of scientific ecology to environmentalism is an important key to bridging past and present, must also remember that "ecology" as a science and "ecology" as the watchword of the environmental movement can have quite different meanings. If I understand ecological scientists correctly, they would regard themselves as investigating an ongoing process in which changing relationships are inevitable. Insofar as it is a natural process, it is quite neutral. Where human actions interfere with the natural process, the results are not automatically harmful, since change will come in one way or another, and they might well be beneficial or certainly tolerable.

My final major dimension of the subject of environmental history is, perhaps something of a catch-all, but I believe it does have a certain unity and does comprehend a group of human responses that are conditioned by the other three categories. It is the sum of all those actions that are taken to regulate the treatment of the natural world in the name of the commonwealth as opposed to what groups or individuals may do in their private capacities. We might label it as the "public" response to environmental concerns, although I think we

generally tend to measure it largely in terms of legis-
lation and the resultant political regulation and en-
forcement of environmental standards. It is, of course,
the aspect of the subject that historians most readily
understand, and a good body of literature exists, especially when we turn to specific issues such as the Progressive Conservation movement of early twentieth-
century America. If we have a problem with this aspect
of the subject, it is simply to keep it in bounds, to
remember how many other forms of thought and action inform the subject, yet not to treat it exclusively in
terms of regulatory laws alone.

My purpose in defining the major components of
environmental history has not been to isolate them per-
manently but rather to identify them more clearly, precisely in order that one might come to understand their
interrelationships more closely and ultimately to integrate them into the single subject of environmental history. Only in that way can we expect to produce a more
balanced and comprehensive understanding of the varied
and complex relationships that have existed throughout
history between human culture and nature. Four disparate
lines of inquiry seem far less likely to achieve that
end. My faith in overly neat schemata is not great, but
in a general way I think it is possible to visualize the
interrelationships of the four categories I have out-
lined: the technological strand, which stands for the
full range of human adaptation to and modification of
the natural environment; the intellectual, which reflects the spectrum of values, attitudes, and ideas that
people have applied to, or derived from, the process of
physical impact; the scientific, or ecological, which
creates a human capacity to perceive and measure the
effect of what humans do to alter nature but which is
also in turn influenced by the climate of thought; and
the public or political, which reveals the manner in
which humans opt to govern their conduct toward nature
in the light of the other three and which in turn affects future applications of technology.

There is a sense in which I am admittedly impos-
ing a rather large demand on my four categories. The
study of each demands the utilization of very different
sources, often employing very different methodologies.

Even if one mortal environmental historian contrives to examine the varied sources, how can he draw his evidence together into the coherent whole I am seeking? I confess I have by no means arrived at an answer. One of the best discussions of the problem, Joseph Petulla's essay in a 1977 issue of Environmental Review, also seems to view the problem as unresolved. I am not even certain that the problem is as yet a pressing one--there seems to be more than enough to do for now in enlarging our fund of evidence and building a basic narrative of environmental history. I would hope, in sum, that the subject will gain methodological rigor simply from a growing body of careful and thoughtful work, but there are advantages in beginning to weigh at least the question of a social context in which to place one's work, a context that has thus far been better supplied by cultural anthropologists than by historians.

However, as John W. Bennett observes in The Ecological Transition: Cultural Anthropology and Human Adaptation, "The majority of cultural ecological studies published to date have been made in socially bounded human communities (tribes, hamlets, ethnic neighborhoods, villages)." Add to this emphasis on very restricted case studies a lack of concern with a longer time span, and such studies have limited use for the historian who is often attempting to survey at least an entire nation over a relatively long time. Bennett is among other things concerned that the ecological transition has led to two contrasting and equally erroneous conceptions: first, an emphasis on environmental determinism with its assumption that nature shapes culture, and, second, the opposing conclusion that as culture developed, humans became entirely independent of nature. With the increasing triumph of the second proposition in human thinking, it became difficult to conceive of a finite or limited environment. As a consequence scholars were more likely to engage in refutations of environmental determinism or investigations of what people did for themselves than to examine the "consequences of an anthropocentric ecological posture and theory." I take Bennett's purpose to be that of finding a way of understanding human environmental relations and their effects on nature more accurately while conceding that nature has been increasingly absorbed in culture--which strikes me as precisely the context in which the student of modern environmental history must work.

There is a sense in which the recent era of environmental history both in the United States and elsewhere generally fits the definition that I have given the subject better than that of earlier periods. Only in recent times have the scientific and technological dimensions of the ecological transition become sufficiently advanced to make possible a precise measurement of the human alteration of the physical environment. But in another sense there is an environmental history of consequence for every age and human group, and the division of that history into technological, intellectual, scientific, and public components is intended to apply universally. For humans have always acted upon the world of nature, have come to understand those actions partly in sensory and intellectual ways and partly by observing their measurable physical impact on nature, and have governed their collective conduct in the light of those perceptions. One might argue that there is a difference only of degree, not of kind, between the hunting culture that comes to understand--or fails to do so--that its game supply is being depleted and the modern, industrial culture that feels itself threatened or benefited by the processes of advanced technology. Even without the completion of the ecological transition--but certainly after it has occurred--what more significant--or more exciting--task awaits the historian than to explore the continuing relationships between humans and nature? One only asks that the environmental historian do so with an awareness of all the dimensions of that relationship, with balance and perspective, and with a sense that it is a relationship that occurs in a social and cultural setting.

ADDENDUM: June 1985

After rereading my essay as originally published, I think I may have been too defensive about the value of treating human relationships with the natural environment as a distinctive and fundamentally important strand of history. I might well begin my discussion more aggressively today, in no small part because I find continuing evidence that too many historians still regard the subject as peripheral rather than recognizing its centrality in a wide range of human activities. I would also argue more emphatically that environmental or ecological history constitutes not so much a "new" approach in history as the recovery of an understanding of a significant aspect of human experience that has operated throughout history but that had become obscured for a few brief centuries as a consequence of a period of rapid technological development in the West.

I would, on the other hand, largely stand by the central arguments of the essay that both the teaching and study of environmental history require close attention to the ongoing interaction between humans and nature that I attempted to define and that a full understanding of this process requires the use of a diverse group of academic disciplines. The complexity of the task, if anything, now seems even greater than I first suggested. Yet, it strikes me that some of the best recent work in the field does, in fact undertake such an approach. There are an increasing number of good examples, although I might especially mention William Cronon, Changes in the Land: Indians, Colonists, and the Ecology of New England (New York, 1983), because in an introductory chapter the author significantly refines my original explanation of the relationship between environment and culture. In stressing the dynamic and changing quality of the interaction between the two and the lack at any time of a stable equilibrium in either, Cronon adds another necessary dimension to the successful study of environmental history.

VI.   THE CONDITION
      OF HISTORY
      IN THE CLASSROOM

ILLUSIONS

Myron A. Marty

September 1978

Readers of this column occasionally ask its editors for their perceptions of the condition of history as an academic discipline in colleges and universities. What's new, they want to know, and what works? Where is the teaching of history headed? When and how will it get there?

Although editing this column compels us to keep up with new ideas and practices in the teaching of history, we claim no special insights regarding these questions. Our perceptions are shaped by what we read, hear, observe, and try in our own classrooms. And because we read, hear, observe, and try different things, neither of us attempts to speak for the other. The comments offered this month are of the "my turn" variety.

I am impressed with the power of the illusions one encounters in analyzing the condition of history in colleges and universities. One must not be too hard on illusions, of course, for illusions undergird the hopes that keep us going in times of adversity. It is desirable, nonetheless, to face up to our illusions from time to time and to ask whether holding to them hinders our work more than it helps. The following illusions, I believe, are the most powerful and most widely shared in historians' circles.

1. THAT THE CURRENT MALAISE IN HIGHER EDUCATION-- THE MALAISE THAT AFFECTS HISTORY AND MOST OTHER DISCI- PLINES--IS TEMPORARY.

Historians, of all people, should know better. A look at some statistics on potential enrollment declines offers the first clue as to what we can expect in the decades ahead. Bureau of Census figures show that the number of eighteen-year-olds in the U.S. population, the traditional source of college freshmen, will peak in 1979 at 4.3 million and decline to a low of 3.2 million

114

in 1992. The only respite in the steady decline in the
pool of potential students will come between 1987 and
1989, too late to reverse the trends set in motion when
enrollment growth began to level off in 1975.

The enrollment decline means that there will be
virtually no infusion of new blood into the teaching
ranks and probably plenty of letting of the old. The
young faculties of the 1960s have matured in the 1970s
and by the 1990s will verge on the aged. A flash-ahead
to the 1990s gives us a glimpse of the survivors of the
decline working with students separated from them in age
by four decades. Age gaps like that are not undesirable
when there is a mix of all ages on the faculty. We do
not know what it will mean when the age balance of this
faculty is so drastically skewed to the elderly. A future article in this column will deal with the changing
attitudes of a faculty member as the shrinkage, coupled
with a decline in basic learning skills of students,
takes place.*

Other aspects of the malaise are equally unprom-
ising. Chronic shortages of money will mean relatively
diminishing salaries, increasing workloads, and deteri-
orating facilities and equipment. I thought about the
effect of these shortages while riding on Amtrak recently. The choice of travel time, I observed, was limited,
the service inefficient, the passengers few, the train
personnel doddering, disinterested and apparently demor-
alized, the cars unkempt, and the tracks in such a state
of disrepair that for long stretches we could not exceed
speeds of ten miles per hour. Parallels in higher education are not hard to imagine.

2. THAT THE CRISIS OF HISTORY IN COLLEGES AND
UNIVERSITIES IS A PASSING ONE.

This illusion lies close to the first one. But
students and dollars tell only part of the story.
Whether anything has happened or is happening to height-
en awareness of the need for integrating knowledge and
understanding of the past into the lives of our citizenry is questionable. For too many people, life is not
even one damn thing after another; rather, as Edna St.
Vincent Millay has put it, "it's one damn thing over and

over." It is hard to teach history to such pastless and futureless people. The apparently growing loss of literacy adds to the problem. And before too many years pass we will have in college classrooms the offspring of parents who cannot remember or even imagine life without television. One cannot help wondering about the future of anything so linear as history with persons whose learning patterns have been shaped so significantly by a nonlinear medium.

History has survived as an academic discipline in many places by settling for smaller pieces of larger and larger pies. If it is to have a future it must find a way of claiming larger pieces of pies that are sure to get smaller and smaller. It is not likely to do this by the reimposition of requirements, no matter how much talk there is about the development of core curricula and finding a place for history in them. The necessary quest for the larger piece of the pie is stymied, however, by other illusions.

3. THAT IT IS POSSIBLE FOR ONE PERSON TO TEACH HISTORY TO ANOTHER.

Although my disagreements with Carl Rogers' approach to counseling are many, I find myself coming back again and again to his "Personal Thoughts on Teaching and Learning," where he writes (with qualifiers interjected along the way): "It seems to me that anything that can be taught to another is relatively inconsequential and has little or no significant influence on behavior . . . . I realize increasingly that I am only interested in learnings which significantly influence behavior . . . . I have come to feel that the only learning which significantly influences behavior is self-discovered, self-appropriated learning. Such self-discovered learning, truth that has been personally appropriated and assimilated in experience, cannot be directly communicated to another." On this point Rogers adds, "As soon as an individual tries to communicate such experience directly, often with a quite natural enthusiasm, it becomes teaching, and its results are inconsequential. It was some relief recently to discover that Soren Kierkegaard . . . had found this too, in his own experience, and stated it very clearly a century ago. It made it seem less absurd."

I have had some good discussions, and I expect to have more, on the question of how the study of history might be expected to influence behavior. This is a matter on which historians are quite naturally of different minds. But we can hardly challenge the notion that self-discovered learning, truth that has been personally appropriated and assimilated in experience, is what we are really aiming for in our students, and that that kind of learning cannot be communicated to them by us. Our preoccupation, unfortunately, has been with teaching rather than learning. We suffer from the illusion, further, that telling is teaching and that teaching is telling. Whether we like it or not, it is not. To foster learning we need to engage in activities that are clearly directed toward that purpose.

4. THAT EFFECTIVE TEACHING METHODS AND STRATEGIES ARE CONTAGIOUS.

In a sense, the reports we have published in this column have nurtured this illusion. They have carried the suggestion that, cast to the wind, the methods and strategies reported on would be seized by eager readers anxious to emulate what good teachers have done to enhance their effectiveness. But are we not all good teachers? Are we not satisfied that our methods are effective, that it is the students' fault that their performance falls so far short of our expectations? Every test, we say, is an assault on our standards. Could it be that that is so because our ineffectiveness limits the students' possibilities of success? Unless we have what some writers have called an "unfreezing experience," we are likely to be immune to new or different ideas, no matter how interestingly they are expressed in this column, in convention sessions, and in other places.

5. THAT NOVELTY IS EXPERIMENT.

Much of what is done by creative, "unfrozen" teachers is called experimental. It is not, it's just different. An experiment requires at least that an attempt be made to measure the effectiveness of the method, strategy, or practice in question. It implies such things as pre-tests, post-tests, and control groups. Such things are largely lacking in the innovative efforts found in history classrooms. Where real experimentation has taken place there have been some interesting discoveries. More such experiments would be desirable, and this column would surely be open to those wishing to report their results here.

6. THAT NEW WAYS ARE BETTER WAYS. THAT OLD WAYS ARE BETTER WAYS.

I have found it interesting that historians, students of change, are so divided on questions of change in history classrooms. To some, change itself is a good thing, something of inherent value. To others, change is decay, a sign of disarray, evidence of compromise, demeaning to the discipline. Those in the second category do not have much to worry about. The changes that have occurred have been minimal and the prospects for further change are probably slight.

It is not change itself, but the nature and purpose of change that matters. At one time I thought it possible to improve the teaching of history, and thus, indirectly, the learning of history, by getting teachers to change their methods. To hope that this might happen, I concluded, is unrealistic. And it is really not too discouraging to settle for helping people to do better what they are already doing. Persons who are basically lecturers, can refine their skills, as can computer users, simulators, role players, and so on.

Change of method, however, is not the only possible kind of change. Curricular change may offer greater possibilities; I shall deal with that in a moment.

7. THAT THERE IS REALLY NOTHING WE CAN DO TO IMPROVE THE STATUS OF HISTORY AS AN ACADEMIC DISCIPLINE.

This illusion is not only discouraging, it is debilitating. Unless we are willing to settle for smaller pieces of smaller pies we must reject it.

There are some things we can do. At the head of

the list should come something called self-assessment.
This column will carry an article in a future issue describing what one department did in a systematic way to
assess its problems, its resources, and its opportunities. Similar self-assessments in departments across
the nation would be highly desirable. They might lead
to the discovery of ways to be more responsive to student interests, to capitalize on new ideas in such
things as material culture and the environment, and to
work around the standard chunking of courses into arti-
ficially constructed periods.

Self-assessment is incomplete if it fails to take
into consideration the nature of the discipline of history and our purposes in teaching it. It does not seem
feasible to insist upon one definition of history's nature and our teaching purposes. What ought to be in-
sisted upon is clarity of definition. Individuals and
departments must compel themselves to hammer through
statements on what they are trying to do and why they
are trying to do it. I am not dismayed by the variety
of definitions such exercises elicit, for history in its
richness allows for such variety. To insist on uniform-
ity and conformity in the profession condemns it to pa-
ralysis. To kill an idea one needs only to insist that
it be refined before it is tried.

It is time, I believe, for teachers of history to
take the offensive, to act instead of merely reacting.
It is time to act, for example, on the issue of what is
called the "new vocationalism." In some institutions,
particularly two-year ones, this might better be called
the "new jobism." The aim of many so called vocational
programs is to equip students with "entry-level skills."
Knowing what we know about such things as the rapid ob-
solescence of classroom-learned skills and the mobility
of persons not only within careers but even in shifting
from career to career, we are doing students an injus-
tice if we do not at least challenge the narrowness of
their training. We have a responsibility to see that
some part of their experiences transcend the training
level. This means that we need to find ways of enlarging
history (or at least humanities) components in vocational programs, not only because that will stabilize
history enrollments and save jobs but because we believe

in the importance of what our discipline has to offer. It follows, of course, that once entry is gained for history in these programs, every muscle must be stretched to make the experiences beneficial to the students. Here is where the imagination and inventiveness of history's practitioners must come into play.

One important point must be recognized in dealing with all questions relating to vocationalism: the essential abilities in all vocations, except, perhaps, for those requiring the narrowest of technical skills, are those of reading, writing, thinking, and problem solving. Historians should not be bashful about their ability to use their discipline as a means for helping students develop these abilities. We should set it as one of our purposes, it seems to me, to help students in precisely this way, no matter how distasteful that suggestion might be to the purists among us.

This is by no means an exhaustive list of the illusions we live with and its suggestions for facing them are all too brief. This article will have served its purpose if it prompts others to identify their lists of illusions and encourages them to come to terms with them as I have sought to do here.

ADDENDUM: May 1985

In September of 1978 Henry Bausum and I were beginning our fifth year as co-editors of "Teaching History Today." In the previous four years we had read and edited many accounts of our fellow historians' efforts to address one problem or another encountered in the classroom. Professor Bausum and I had corresponded at length about these efforts, and we had discussed them frequently on the phone. The condition of history in the classroom seemed to be worsening, with no prospects of improvement in sight. One reason, we felt, was that illusions hampered efforts to accomplish changes, and we agreed that I should attempt to identify and elaborate briefly on these illusions.

Looking back seven years, I have no reason to believe either that the 1978 essay missed the mark or that by 1985 the illusions of which I wrote have vanished.

Renewed efforts to make the most of every opportunity presenting itself to teachers of history must be seized if constructive change is to occur.

----

*The article referred to on page 114, "Teaching History: A Mid-Career Reappraisal," was submitted by Thomas M. Canfield and was published in November 1978.

NOTES ON CONTRIBUTORS

Jacqueline B. Barnhart is Professor of History at California State University, Chico. Her column in this collection describes an oral history project. Her research has been primarily in social history, and a forthcoming publication, Fair but Frail, Prostitution in San Francisco 1849-1900, is to be published by the University of Nevada.

Henry S. Bausum is Professor of History and former Chairman of the Department of History and Politics at the Virginia Military Institute. He was one of the co-editors of "Teaching History Today" from its inception to 1981.

E. Bradford Burns is Professor of History at the Universty of California, Los Angeles. He based the column reprinted in this collection on a speech which he delivered as Dean of the Division of Honors at UCLA to a meeting of the chairs of history departments from colleges and universities in the state of California.

Patricia B. Ebrey is Associate Professor of History in the Center for East Asian and Pacific Studies at the University of Illinois at Urbana-Champaign. Her work on a sourcebook--since published by Free Press under the title, Chinese Civilization and Society: A Sourcebook--resulted in her submission of the column reprinted in this collection.

Evelyn Edson is Professor of History at Piedmont Virginia Community College. She was inspired and, as she puts it, infuriated by the American Historical Review article on Western Civilization authored by Gilbert Allerdyce. She is particularly appreciative of her own training in Western Civilization at The University of Chicago, and yet aware of the ill-preparation of teachers of Western Civilization.

Norman A. Graebner is Edwin R. Stettinus Professor of American Diplomatic History at the University of Virginia. He is the author of many works in American Diplomatic History. He was one of the recipients of the first teaching awards offered at the University of Illinois and the paper published in the 1975 "Teaching History Today" column reflects the thought he gave to teaching at that time.

Julie Thompson Klein is Professor of Humanities at Wayne State University. Her column for "Teaching History Today" came about as a result of her involvement in an interdisciplinary program in which strong emphasis is placed on historical and cultural awareness. She has published widely on interdisciplinary theory and method and is currently completing a book on the concept of interdisciplinarity.

Gerda Lerner was on the faculty of Sarah Lawrence College when she wrote her 1976 column for "Teaching History Today." She was the founder and co-director of the M.A. program in Women's History at Sarah Lawrence. She is now Robinson-Edwards Professor of History and Senior Distinguished Research Professor at the University of Wisconsin--Madison. In addition to many books on women's history, she is the author of the AHA pamphlet Teaching Women's History and has been influential in bringing about the orderly and successful expansion of women's history programs in the past decade.

Myron A. Marty was Professor of History at St. Louis Community College at Florissant Valley when the column reprinted here was published. He is now Dean of the College of Liberal Arts and Sciences at Drake University. He was one of the original coeditors of "Teaching History Today," has published widely on subjects related to the teaching of history, and served for several years as Deputy Director in the Division of Education Programs at the National Endowment for the Humanities. At the time of this writing he is a nominee for Vice President of the Teaching Division of the AHA.

William H. McNeill is Robert A. Millikan Distinguished Service Professor of History at The University of Chicago and is currently President of the American Historical Association. He was the AHA council member in charge of the transition in 1974 from the AHA Committee on Teaching to the present AHA Teaching Division with a vice president sitting on the AHA council. He is largely responsible for establishing "Teaching History Today" as a regular column and is author of many books of which The Rise of the West and World History have a direct bearing on the teaching of history.

John E. O'Connor is Professor of History at the New Jersey Institute of Technology. He has been influential in stirring interest in the teaching of history, perhaps most noticeably as editor since its inception of Film and History and as co-author of the AHA pamphlet, Teaching History with Film.

E.A. Reitan is Professor and past Chairman of the Department of History at Illinois State University, Normal. He has been active in matters relating to teaching as co-author of a textbook, English History, by Forum Press, and as member and former chairman of the AHA Robinson Prize Committee award for the best textbook or teaching aid in history.

Lester D. Stephens is professor and head of the Department of History at the University of Georgia. He served as consultant to many secondary school programs in the social studies and directed a course on methods of teaching the social studies. From that activity came a book, Probing the Past: A Guide to the Study and Teaching of History (1974), and the article which he wrote for "Teaching History Today" in 1977.

Thad W. Tate is director of the Institute of Early American History and Culture at the College of William and Mary. His column for "Teaching History Today" followed his preparation of a paper on teaching environmental history for a session of the American Historical Association. The session was organized by the American Society for Environmental History.

APPENDIX

Following is a list of the "Teaching History Today" columns published since September 1974. During the autumn, 1974, the column appeared under the title, "Innovation in Undergraduate History" and during the first year of its existence each column included remarks from several persons. Accordingly, I enter below only the authors and their college/university affiliation for the columns during that year. Beginning with the academic year 1975-76, the column took on its present shape and so I indicate the author and title.

1974-1975

September: Nancy Weiss, Princeton Univ., and Daniel P. Resnick, Carnegie-Mellon

October: Matthew T. Downey, Univ. of Colorado, John G. Gagliardo, Boston Univ., David D. Buck, Univ. of Wisconsin, Milwaukee, and Wallace T. MacCaffrey, Harvard Univ.

November: Steven Frick, Earlham Col., C. Stewart Doty, Univ. of Maine, Orono, and David D. Buck, Univ. of Wisconsin, Milwaukee

December: Carolyn C. Lougee, Stanford Univ., Noel R. Miner, Univ. of Colorado, and William B. Wheeler, Univ. of Tennessee

January: Robert H. Keller, Jr., Fairhaven Col., Sidney M. Bolkosky, Univ. of Michigan, Dearborn, and John Scarborough, Univ. of Kentucky

February: Ted L. Underwood, Univ. of Minnesota-Morris, E. Bradford Burns, UCLA, Samuel Lieberstein, Temple Univ., William R. Cook, State Univ. of New York-Geneseo, and Rudolph Heinze, Concordia Teachers Col.

March: Robert V. Schnucker, Northeast Missouri

State Univ., Paul Devendittis, Nassau Community Col., Philip H. Niles & Kirk Jeffrey, Carleton Col., and Mel Steely, West Georgia Col.

April:

Jo Ann Hutchinson & Gerald Greer, Forrest High School, Oak Park, Ill., Myron Marty, Florissant Valley Community Col., and Frederic A. Youngs, Jr., Louisiana State Univ.

May:

Richard C. Raack, California State Univ.-Hayward, Susan Armitage, Univ. of Colorado, and John H. Gauger, Lehigh Community Col.

1975-1976

September:

Bausum and Marty, editors of "Teaching History Today."

October:

Charles F. Sidman, "Report on the Kansas Plan."

November:

Stephen R. Graubard, "Difficulties Facing Higher Education."

December:

Norman A. Graebner, "Observations on University Teaching and Research."

January:

Robert A. Waller, "An Historical Skills Approach in the U.S. History Survey."

February:

J. William T. Youngs, Jr., "The Bicentennial in the Classroom."

March:

William H. McNeill, "History for Citizens."

April:

Bruce Mazlish, "On Teaching History."

May:

Gerda Lerner, "Teaching Women's History."

1976-1977

September: Myron Marty, "Thinking about Teaching."

October: B. Lee Cooper, "Teaching American History through Popular Music."

November: George E. Hopkins, "Assassination as History: An Analysis of the Uses of an Experimental 'Mini-course' Format."

December: Barry K. Beyer, "Improving Undergraduate History Teaching: The Potential and Limitations of P.S.I."

January: Maxine Seller, "The Training of the College History Teacher: A Teaching Division Survey."

February: Thomas J. Schlereth, "The City as Artifact."

March: John E. O'Connor, "Film Study and the History Classroom."

April: Lester D. Stephens, "From History to Social Studies."

May: Judith Zinsser Lippman, "World History at the United Nations International School."

1977-1978

September: Henry Bausum, "The Social Function of History."

October: Robert G. Shafer, "Computer in the (History) Classroom."

November: Robert S. Feldman, "Historical Role Playing: An Alternative Teaching Strategy."

December: "Two Project Reports: 'Experiments

in History Teaching,' 'OAH History Education Center.'"

January: Carl G. Gustavson, "The Historiography of Blue Books."

February: John E. Wills, Jr., "History and its Audience: A Course and a Concept."

March: John M. McKenna, "Original Historical Manuscripts and the Undergraduate."

April: E. A. Reitan, "New Perspectives on Using the Library in History Teaching."

May: Neil J. O'Connell, "Toward A World History."

1978-1979

September: Myron A. Marty, "Illusions."

October: Stuart R. Givens & James L. Litwin, "A Strategy for Renewal: Active Departmental Self-Study."

November: Thomas M. Camfield, "Teaching History: A Mid-Career Reappraisal."

December: Ross W. Beales, "Historians and the NEH Summer Seminars."

January: Robert V. Schnucker, "What's Wrong with History Teaching?"

February: Marilyn E. Weigold, "Lab Work for History Students."

March: Kenneth P. Werrell, "History and Fiction: Challenge and Opportunity," and Mark Elliott, "Asking Students 'How Historical is Zola's Germinal?'"

April: Jerry Israel, "Midwestern Small Cities: Building an Integrated Social Science

Curriculum."

May: David Strauss, "Comparative History in
                the Classroom."

1979-1980

September: Gordon R. Mork, "Teaching History with
                Games."

October: Charles W. Connell, "Attitude and De-
                velopment as Factors in the Learning of
                History: The Work of William Perry."

November: Robert E. Roeder, "The Twentieth Centu-
                ry World: An Experience in Course De-
                velopment."

December: Marvin Lunenfeld, "A Nice Place to
                Visit: Teaching Urban Civilization Out-
                side of the Classroom."

January: James C. Williams, "So You've Got Some
                Old Ruins--Now What?"

February: Fay D. Metcalf and Matthew T. Downey,
                "Do School History Textbooks Lie to
                Children? Reflections on Frances Fitz-
                Gerald's America Revised."

March: G. Wesley Johnson, Peter Stearns, and
                Joel A. Tarr, "Public History: A New
                Area of Teaching, Research, and Employ-
                ment."

April: DeLloyd J. Guth, "History as Epistemol-
                ogy."

May: Myron Marty, "Measuring the Stirrings
                of Change in the Teaching of History."

1980-1981

September: No Column.

October: John Anthony Scott, "Lowen V. Turnip-seed: A Landmark Case."

November: Patricia Ebrey, "Using Primary Sources in Teaching Social History."

December: Jacqueline B. Barnhart, "Doing Oral History: The Yountville Project."

January: Warren Leon, "Fear of Tripping or De-signing a College Field Trip That Works."

February: Earl P. Bell, Jr., "Alternative Ap-proaches for Curriculum in American History: An Annual Workshop for Teach-ers in Secondary Schools."

March: Linda W. Rosenzweig and Peter Stearns, "Social History for the High Schools."

April: No Column.

May: Thad W. Tate, "Problems of Definition in Environmental History."

1981-1982

September: No Column.

October: Richard K. Liberman, "History in the Community."

November: Lawrence B. Davis, "A New Perspective on American History."

December: James B. Crooks, "Another Perspective on History Enrollments."

January: Julie Thompson Klein, "To Begin With... Exercises in Historiography."

February: William L. Burton, "The Use and Abuse of History."

March: Mildred Alpern, "Modernization and Social History."

April: No Column.

May: David Felix, "Revitalizing the Teaching of History in New York City: A University-Public School Joint Undertaking."

1982-1983

September: Steven A. Riess, "Sport History in the Classroom."

October: Mary L. Lifka, "History as a Genre."

November: No Column.

December: Brian C. Mitchell, "Teaching Local History: Lowell and the Adult Evening Experience."

January: E. Bradford Burns, "Teaching History: A Changing Clientele and an Affirmation of Goals."

February: Kim Phillips, "Some Thoughts on American History Textbooks."

March: Richard Place and Christopher Johnson, "Teaching History to Social Work Students."

April: Francis Jennings, "The Newberry Library Center for the History of the American Indian: Its Impact on School and Community Constituencies."

May: Michael D'Innocenzo, Martin Melkonian, and Sandra Mullin, "Special Studies in History: War and Peace in a Nuclear Age."

1983-1984

September: Christine Naitove and Barbara Bartle, "A European History Course that Stresses Writing and Reasoning Skills."

October: Terry A. Cooney, "Drawing History: Working with Student Attitudes from the First Day."

November: David L. Porter, "Debating the Great Historical Issues."

December: John J. Appel, "Postcards: More Than Just 'Wish You Were Here.'"

January: No Column.

February: Evelyn Edson, "Reflections on the History of Western Civilization: An Unblushing Apology, or Perhaps a Love Letter."

March: Virginia S. Wilson, James A. Litle, and Gerald L. Wilson, "Blending the Two Cultures: The Role of History and the Social Sciences in the Education of Future Scientific/Technological Leaders."

April: No Column.

May: Fraser Harbutt, "A Course on the History of U.S.-Soviet Relations."